SUCCESSFULLY GROW & GARDEN CITRUS FRUIT TREES USING POTS & CONTAINERS

BEGINNER'S GUIDE TO SELECTING THE RIGHT TREE, POTS AND CONTAINERS FOR INDOOR AND OUTDOOR, PESTS AND DISEASES, TRANSPLANTING AND ESPALIER

MADISON PIERCE

CONTENTS

INTRODUCTION

One of the biggest challenges faced by newbies to the world of citrus gardening is a lack of experience. Without the knowledge and know-how required, most beginner citrus fruit gardeners give up too soon, usually because their plants become unhappy or plagued by pests. Sometimes citrus fruit gardening can seem a lot more complicated than it is. Armed with the right advice and guidance, you can have a citrus fruit tree garden that doesn't only produce the sweet reward of quality fruit but absolutely thrives year in and year out.

Many avid gardeners discover that growing fruit trees directly in the ground presents various difficult to overcome complexities. For this reason, this entire book focuses on how to effectively (and most successfully) grow strong, sturdy citrus fruit trees in pots and containers which produce fruit bountifully.

By now you're probably wondering who I am and what makes me an authority on the subject of citrus container gardening. I will start by telling you that my name is Madison Peirce. I wrote this book to help avid gardeners and sustainable lifestyle enthusiasts grasp the concept, theories, and practical applications of growing fruit at home.

I am a devoted wife and mother, and to say that I am a fruit tree enthusiast would be an understatement. I live and breathe gardening, and one of my main focus areas is fruit trees. Whenever someone sees and samples the fruit from my garden, they marvel at just how much effort must have gone into nurturing and growing them.

While I admit that a considerable amount of heart and soul has gone into my garden, it was a process to get the basics down to a fine art. Ever since I equipped myself with practical gardening knowledge, the process has been more straightforward than expected and immensely rewarding. I share my wealth of citrus fruit tree gardening knowledge and experience with other passionate gardeners because I want like-minded people to derive the same joy I have from the process.

Growing up in sunny South Africa and spending most of my life living and traveling abroad, I have come to understand the challenges imposed on fruit trees in varying climates and just how rewarding and convenient container gardening can be. As a devoted mother and wife, I love the fact that we can enjoy fresh, healthy fruit plucked from our very own fruit trees – there's something so *wholesome* about that.

Enough about me though; let's focus our attention on citrus tree container gardening.

There are several crucial elements to growing and nurturing exceptional citrus trees. First and foremost, it's about getting to know what citrus trees like and dislike. Just like you and me, trees have their lifestyle preferences, so it stands to reason that if you give your trees what they want and need most, they will reward you with an abundance of fruit. It's important to note that you will reap the rewards of the time, effort, and care you put in. At this point, educating yourself is of the utmost importance.

Great care is taken to impart valuable information on how to successfully plant, nurture, grow, and eat from your potted citrus trees. You'll also learn techniques to overcome the challenges of growing fruit trees indoors and how to determine what is wrong with your tree when it's looking unwell or not producing as expected. Here you will learn simple and effective methods of rectifying problems and enriching the life of your plant. I also provide step-by-step guidance on how to transplant your thriving potted fruit trees into the garden. And finally, the fine art of Espalier growing is touched on.

We will thoroughly scrutinize the ins and outs of container gardening and tweak the process to tend to the needs of thriving fruit trees specifically. You can expect to explore all of the concepts below in the following chapters:

- Choosing the right indoor fruit tree for you
- Selecting a suitable pot or container
- Planting techniques, including soil preparation
- Tips for citrus fruit tree growing (watering, temperatures, pest control, etc.)
- Instructions for fruit tree nurturing and maintenance
- Telltale signs of problems and how to rectify them
- Transitioning your growing tree to the garden

There's a lot more to citrus container gardening than simply popping a seedling into a pot and letting it grow. Because of this, learning various simple yet effective strategies for growing suitably sized, manageable, and high-yield fruit trees is the focus of this book.

There are several things you should acquire before you get started:

- Gardening gloves (choose a pair that fits snugly)
- Pruners
- Watering can
- Gardening boots/shoes (preferably waterproof) for when the transplanting takes place

Let's pull on our gardening gloves and get to work achieving what we set out to do: to successfully grow and nurture high-yield citrus fruit trees. Please join our community of avid gardeners for useful tips and information on all things gardening by scanning the QR code below.

SELECTING THE RIGHT INDOOR CITRUS FRUIT TREE

When you start container gardening, it's good to know what your options are. I have found that some citrus fruit trees thrive in containers, and those are the ones on which we will focus. This section introduces citrus fruit tree options, their individual "personalities", and what makes them a viable choice for your citrus container gardening project. Attention is also given to common pests and diseases for each type of tree to have an idea of what challenges you will face. Our focus will be on the following fruit trees:

1. Kumquats
2. Lemons

3. Sweet Limes / Limes
4. Oranges
5. Mandarins

INTRODUCING THE 5 BEST FRUIT TREE SPECIES FOR INDOOR CONTAINER GARDENING

Enter the spotlight, my favorite selection of fruit trees! I *know* these trees do well in an indoor, container-growing environment, so there's every reason to try these out as a beginner. Of course, all plants have their challenges to overcome. Once you understand the tree and the risks that it faces, you will be able to approach gardening, nurturing, and maintaining your tree with confidence (and efficiency, mind you).

Let's get to know our feature fruit trees below.

1. KUMQUATS

Germination Time	2 – 4 weeks
Days to Harvest	Up to 90 days to form fruit
Size	8ft high – 6ft wide (2.4m high – 1.8m wide)
Light Requirements	6 – 8 hours of sunlight a day – position near the window
Repotting	Every 2 years
Temperature Tolerances	Thrives in high temperatures but also survives in low temperatures of 44 degrees Fahrenheit (-7 degrees Celsius)

Kumquats are trees native to eastern Asia. Nowadays, they are commonly found in the United States and various countries with a warm climate. The name translates to "Golden Orange" in English. They are a group of reasonably small citrus trees that form part of the Rutaceae family. Kumquat trees are commonly grown in many countries and regions, including Brazil, Israel, Peru, Indonesia, China, Japan, California, Florida, Indochina, and the Mediterranean.

The Kumquat fruit is grape-sized with 3 – 6 segments, and the flavor is a combination of sweet and tart. The fruit, with edible skin, is jam-packed with Vitamin C and Omega-3 fats, so it's excellent for getting some extra goodness into a diet.

The flower of the Kumquat tree is delicate and white with either a white or pale-yellow center.

Something to note is that Kumquat trees are self-pollinating, so you could start with just one tree and work your way up from there. The tree will require moist soil, so you will have to water it regularly to ensure that the roots don't dry out. They also like their fertilizer, so be prepared to provide that.

Types of Kumquats for Indoor Growing

Having worked with Kumquat trees before, I would recommend focusing on the variants that respond well to indoor growing. There are three variants of Kumquats that are good options as long as you ensure that they are positioned in a well-lit spot if you are growing them indoors. These are as follows:

Fukushu

This Kumquat species has a slightly sweeter-than-normal fruit and has thornless growth. You will find that the leaves of the Fukushu Kumquat tree are larger than most other Kumquat species. This particular species is considered a high-yield tree. Because it is slow-growing and compact, it's also known as a natural dwarf – making it a perfect choice for container gardeners looking for an ornamental tree.

The Fukushu Kumquat tree produces slightly larger fruit than other varieties. The fruit has a somewhat different oval shape, and in addition to this, the skin is thinner than other Kumquat fruits. If you're keen on growing ornamental fruit trees, the Fukushu Kumquat tree fits the bill.

Meiwa

This Kumquat variety is the sweetest and least seedy of all the Kumquat species with minimal thorny growth. The Meiwa tree is a hybrid of Nagami and Marumi Kumquats and produces a plump round fruit. This is a less common variety of Kumquat trees with sweet fruit (less tart than most other varieties) and thicker skin than the Fukushu Kumquat. What's interesting about the Meiwa Kumquat is that it's a semi-dormant tree in winter, which leads to it effectively withstanding temperatures that drop below freezing. I have found that not many citrus trees are tolerant of cold, so I find this quite an attractive "personality trait" of the Meiwa. This Kumquat tree is less ornamental than the Fukushu Kumquat but is still considered a decorative option.

Tavares Limequat

The Tavares Limequat is a fruit that's a cross between a Mexican Lime and a Kumquat. The Tavares tree is one of the most attractive Kumquat varieties and is a popular choice because it is naturally compact. The Tavares Limequat grows to less than 6ft (1.8m) tall when it is fully matured and has foliage quite similar to mandarin oranges.

The tree also presents attractive small white flowers when in bloom. The Tavares Limequat is a tad smaller than the Mexican Lime and somewhat sweeter when it comes to flavor and size. As a hybrid, the tree does well in colder temperatures. In fact, if it's well protected, it can withstand temperatures as low as 32 degrees Fahrenheit (0 degrees Celsius).

Kumquat Common Pests & Diseases

Just like any plant, pests and diseases like to target Kumquats. There's good news, though. You can prepare to overcome the problem and ensure your fruit tree's long-term health by knowing the risks. Below we list some of the pests and diseases that target Kumquats. You can find more in-depth information on each pest/disease, preventative measures, and treatments in Chapter Six.

PESTS THAT TARGET KUMQUATS

- Mealybugs
- Leaf miners
- Citrus scale
- Aphids

Diseases that plague Kumquats

- Alternaria Leaf Spots
- Anthracnose

Interestingly, Kumquat trees are Citrus Canker resistant.

2. LEMONS

Germination Time	1 – 3 weeks
Days to Harvest	4 – 12 months
Size	3 – 10ft (1 – 3m) in a container
Light Requirements	6 – 8 hours of sunlight a day – position near the window
Repotting	Every 2 –3 years
Temperature Tolerances	Thrives in temperatures of 77 – 86 degrees Fahrenheit (25 – 30 degrees Celsius) and can withstand temperatures of no less than 32 degrees Fahrenheit (0 degrees Celsius)

Lemon trees are also part of the Rutaceae family of citrus trees. They are commonly grown in the USA, Italy, Spain, Mexico, and Argentina. Therefore, it's not too surprising that Lemon trees prefer warm climates, and if exposed to temperatures below 32 degrees Fahrenheit (0 degrees Celsius), their leaves drop off, and the tree withers and dies. Choosing container gardening for your Lemon trees will enable you to shift them indoors during the colder months. One of the top benefits of citrus container gardening is protecting your trees from the cold and ensuring that you have finite control over soil conditions.

Types of Lemons for Container Gardening

The type of Lemon tree you choose to grow will determine how big it gets and how much it produces when planted in a container. I recommend choosing between the following three varieties, with which I have had great personal success.

Meyer Lemons

Take the time to note the Meyer Lemons variations when buying seedlings and seeds or even when buying a grown plant. The "Improved Meyer" Lemon is considered the ideal variety for container gardeners who live in cooler areas. Meyer Lemons are a fun Lemon tree that's always blossoming and bearing fruit.

The flowers of this tree are delicate and white with a yellow center. Initially in China, Meyer Lemon trees were popular for their ornamental properties and not always for being edible. It is said that Martha Stewart made Meyer Lemons a cooking household name with her recipes in the 1990s.

Many newbies find growing this variant a rewarding option because it can be brought indoors during winter without sacrificing fruit production. Growing a Lemon tree indoors and getting a healthy harvest from it is like winning first prize!

That said, the reason behind the tree being called the "Improved Meyer" Lemon tree is because it is a disease-free variant of the regular Meyer Lemon, which is a lovely type of Lemon, by the way. The fruit features pale yellow inside flesh in 10 – 12 segments, with a moderately acidic taste. The lemons are typically smaller and rounder than regular lemons and have a thin skin that is smooth and ranges from deep yellow to orange.

However, the Improved Meyer Lemon tree produces a sweeter fruit (that lacks the Lemon tang) with even thinner skin. You may also find it interesting that it's a lemon-orange hybrid.

Sungold Lemons

Sungold Lemon trees seem to be growing in popularity, mainly for their striking appearance; however, they can be pretty rare to get your hands on. What makes the Sungold Lemon so eye-catching is that its fruit is bright green and yellow striped, and the leaves variegated. Something that endears Sungold Lemons to me is that their leaves are fragrant (almost zesty) if you crush them or brush past them. The tree itself has spines and thorns, so use caution when working with a Sungold Lemon tree.

What sets the Sungold Lemon apart from other Lemons is how it carries its green stripes through its leaves *and* rind. In some Lemons, this is a sign of nutrient deficiency, but in the Sungold Lemon, it's not. It's just a sign of a happy, fun Lemon fruit!

When you get to know the Sungold Lemon, you will find that it prefers warm temperatures of 77 – 86 degrees Fahrenheit (25 – 30 degrees Celsius) but is hardy enough to survive temperatures that drop as low as 50 degrees Fahrenheit (10 degrees Celsius). When growing indoors, you can expect your tree to do well even at lower temperatures, which is good news.

A pair of thick gloves will come in handy when working with Sungold Lemons as their thorns can be quite devilish.

Variegated Pink Lemons

Another Lemon tree popular for its appearance is the Variegated Pink Lemon tree, which is most popularly grown in Southern California. That said, with container gardening, the Variegated Pink Lemon tree can do well anywhere. This variant is also often called the Pink-Fleshed Eureka, and it is pretty hard not to notice.

The 10 – 12 segmented fruit owes its pink hue to the presence of lycopene, which is the same compound that colors tomatoes. Much like the Sungold Lemon, this variant has green and white striped leaves, green striped fruit rind, and very fragrant foliage. The stripes tend to become more visible as the fruit ripens.

The unique pink color of the flesh causes a lot of interest in the tree, so if you're looking to grow something a little different, this one's for you. A new Variegated Pink Lemon tree will take 4 – 5 years to produce its first crop, usually harvested in the summer.

The flavor of this Lemon will undoubtedly get your lips puckering. The fruit is typically tart, but the good news is that it becomes less acidic as it matures – in the end, the mature fruit is slightly less sour and tart than a regular lemon. Note that Variegated Pink Lemons do *not* like frost at all, so don't risk leaving the tree outside during the cooler months.

Lemon Tree Common Pests & Diseases

Pests and diseases will rob you of your fruit tree gardening efforts if you aren't aware of the risks and ready to take action. Lemon trees attract quite a few diseases and insect infestations. Below we list the most common pests and diseases that target Lemon trees. More in-depth information on identification, preventative measures, and treatments are in Chapter Six.

Pests that Target Lemon Trees

- Thrips
- Aphids
- Scale Insects
- Leaf Miners

Diseases that Target Lemon Trees

Of course, it's not always insects that attack Lemon trees. Diseases can also plague the health of your tree. Below are a few of which to be aware.

- European Brown Rot
- Greasy Spot
- Citrus Canker

- Sooty Mold Fungus
- Anthracnose

3. SWEET LIMES / LIMES

Germination Time	3 – 6 weeks
Days to Harvest	3 – 4 years
Size	6 – 7 ft (1.8 – 2.1m) in a container
Light Requirements	6 – 8 hours of sunlight a day – position near the window
Repotting	Every 3 – 4 years
Temperature Tolerances	Thrives in temperatures of 77 – 86 degrees Fahrenheit (25 – 30 degrees Celsius) and can withstand temperatures of no less than 50 degrees Fahrenheit (10 degrees Celsius)

Sweet Limes, commonly referred to as Indian Sweet Limes, Palestine Sweet Limes, or Mausambi, are native to India and make for the perfect container citrus tree because they don't grow very tall. In a container, Sweet Lime trees don't get much taller than 6 – 7 ft (1.8 – 2.1 m). Like most citrus trees, Sweet Limes prefer a warm, sunny climate and are self-pollinating.

Sweet Lime trees are commercially grown in Northern India and Egypt but are popular garden plants in many countries across the world. In India, the tree is often used as a rootstock (rootstock is a plant used for grafting another plant). It is eaten prolifically in Palestine.

When getting to know your Sweet Lime tree's preferences, you will find that it requires protection from cold snaps but is otherwise a reasonably hardy citrus tree that doesn't require too much care to survive and thrive.

The Indian Sweet Lime has pure white flowers and fruit that is small, round, and often faintly ribbed (this happens rarely). When mature, the fruit has a smooth rind that is pale green to yellow-orange. Inside, the fruit is pale yellow and juicy with seeds. When it comes to taste, Sweet Limes are less acidic than regular limes and have a sweeter flavor.

Sweet Lime / Lime Tree Pests & Diseases

If you want to take care of your Limes, it is essential to familiarize yourself with pests and diseases that plague them. It's good to educate yourself on the risks to ensure that you're able to identify them, prevent them, and rid your tree of them when/if they do arrive. While the most common pests and diseases of Lime trees are mentioned below, more in-depth information in Chapter Six teaches how to identify, prevent, and treat against them.

Pests that Target Sweet Limes / Limes

- Leaf Miners
- Aphids
- Scale Insects
- Citrus Mites

Diseases that Target Sweet Limes / Limes

- Black Sooty Mold
- Citrus Canker
- Phytophthora Fungus
- Anthracnose

4. ORANGES

Germination Time	6 – 8 weeks
Days to Harvest	7 – 12 months
Size	6ft (1.8m) in a container
Light Requirements	6 – 8 hours of sunlight a day – position near the window
Repotting	Every 3 – 4 years
Temperature	Thrives in temperatures of 59 – 98 degrees
Tolerances	Fahrenheit (15 – 37 degrees Celsius) and can withstand temperatures of no less than 28 degrees Fahrenheit (-2 degrees Celsius)

Oranges, which form part of the Rutaceae family, are a top choice of citrus tree for container gardening. Their ornamental appearance and high Vitamin C content make them a popular choice.

Oranges originate from Asia, more particularly from the Malay Archipelago region. Currently, Orange trees are grown successfully in the USA, Australia, eastern Mediterranean countries, and South Africa. Of course, oranges thrive in a warm climate, but that doesn't mean that you can't grow an orange tree very successfully wherever you are in the world (thanks to container gardening).

Types of Oranges Best Suited to Container Gardening

Choosing the correct type of Orange tree for your container gardening project will make all the difference to your success. There are three types of oranges that I genuinely enjoy growing for their ease of care. I have also found that these specific orange trees provide rewarding harvests when they get what they want and need. It's a great idea to choose one of the following Orange trees for your container gardening project.

Calamondin

There is something extraordinary about the Calamondin Orange, in my opinion. Not only is it an attractive tree to grow with its miniature 6 – 10 segmented oranges, but it also has a different taste to most Oranges, similar to a toned-down lemon taste. Because the taste is unexpected for an Orange, the fruit is used for jams and preserves.

The leaves of the Calamondin Orange are glossy dark green on the top and yellow-green underneath. The flowers, which are slightly larger than most typical citrus flowers, are bright white and highly fragrant. These particular oranges are quite hardy in cold environments, although, like all citrus trees, they do prefer warmer climates. One of the advantages of gardening Calamondins indoors is that you can provide them with the climate conditions they prefer.

Something that I have found quite remarkable about growing Calamondin Oranges is that it produces mature fruit year-round. Most fruit takes approximately one year to ripen, which means that the tree is serving as a highly ornamental focal point inside or outside the home for the majority of the year. Functional and eye-catching – it sounds like the perfect tree, doesn't it?!

This Orange is native to the Philippines, Borneo, Indonesia, China, and Taiwan and goes by many different names, including Calamansi, Philippine Lemon, and Philippine Lime. The tree was first mentioned in the USA in 1900 as an "Acid Orange". It's often chosen as a patio plant or trimmed into a thick hedge.

Calamondin fruits only grow to around 0.13ft (4cm) in diameter with an extremely fine skin that loosens as the fruit matures. A Calamondin tree grown in a container will only reach 3 – 6 ½ ft (91cm – 198cm) tall. If you choose this tree, prepare to repot it every 2 – 3 years just after the fruit formation period.

Navel Oranges (Washington and Robertson)

Navel Oranges are another popular type of Orange tree for container gardening. I have had particular success with both the Washington and Robertson Navel Orange trees. Naturally, I strongly recommend both of these types of Orange trees to beginners.

You will find that the Washington and Robertson Navel Oranges are almost identical, except for the fact that Robertson variants produce fruit at least two weeks earlier than the Washington variant. Here's a nice tip for those who love snacking on Oranges; if you grow one of each tree, you can harvest for a more extended period each year (which means more fruit for you).

Navel Oranges are popular for several reasons, over and above the fact that they are easy to care for and grow. For instance, Washington Navel Oranges produce substantial fruits (with 10 – 12 segments) with easy-peeling loose skin. The taste of the Orange is sweet and juicy and conveniently seedless too.

Robertson Navel Oranges are also very popular for their loose skin and seedless, sweet-tasting fruit. One of the drawcards for focusing on this type of Navel Orange is that it's a naturally dwarf variant that grows into a bushy, shrub-like tree. When you get to know your Navel Orange tree a bit better, you will discover that the harvests can be pretty vast when it starts to produce fruit.

Tarocco

The Tarocco Orange is close to my heart because it's got an air of mystery to it. While it is Orange for all intents and purposes, it has a deep red, seedless flesh leading to its nickname, "Blood Orange". Of course, the mystery of the Tarocco's deep red is not really a mystery. It is due to high anthocyanin content, a powerful antioxidant that can create a deep red-orange appearance.

The succulent red flesh has 10 – 12 easily detachable segments and a loose protective skin that is easy to peel. The flowers of the Tarocco are delicate and small against dark green leaves, making them stand out. If anything, this particular Orange tree is worth having a second glance at!

The Tarocco Orange is native to Italy, and some even say that the name comes from a farmer who first discovered it and claimed it is "Tarocco", which in Italian means "Fraud". In addition to its unusual appearance for an orange, the Tarocco Orange's flavor is aptly described as "complex" with distinct raspberry overtones.

If you're interested in Espalier growing, the Tarocco makes an excellent option for it, but we will cover this a little further on in this book.

Orange Tree Pests & Diseases

Some common diseases and pests attack orange trees – it's best to be aware of them. Listed below are both diseases and pests, but more in-depth information on recognizing, preventing, and treating them is in Chapter Six.

Pests that Target Orange Trees

- Anthracnose
- Armillaria Root Rot
- Black Root Rot
- Blast
- Citrus Canker
- Phytophthora Gummosis
- Aphids
- Mealybugs
- Scales
- Snails
- Leaf miners

5. MANDARINS

Germination Time	7 – 10 days
Days to Harvest	4 – 7 years
Size	6 – 7 ft (1.8 – 2.1m) in a container
Light Requirements	8 hours min of sunlight a day – position near the window
Repotting	Every 2 – 3 years
Temperature	Thrives in temperatures of 59 – 89 degrees
Tolerances	Fahrenheit (15 – 32 degrees Celsius) and can withstand temperatures of no less than 22 degrees Fahrenheit (-5.5 degrees Celsius)

Mandarins are technically a type of Orange and are often chosen for citrus container gardening because they prove simple to care for and simple to grow. Mandarin trees originate from the Philippines and Southeast Asia. They are primarily grown in China, India, East Indies, Australia, and Japan. With the right approach and know-how, you can grow a Mandarin tree almost anywhere.

The fruit is often referred to as "kid-glove oranges" because the skin is loose and easy to peel, and the segments are easy to pull apart without damaging the fruit.

The Mandarin's skin is fragile, and the fruit, which grows on a thorny tree, looks similar to a small, squashed orange with red-orange flesh inside.

When it comes to getting to know your Mandarin tree and what it likes (and dislikes), you will find that they are typical citrus trees. This means that they love a lot of light and sunshine, need a moderate water supply, and if given what they want and need, they thrive with relative ease.

Types of Mandarins Best Suited to Container Gardening

You may find it interesting that Mandarins include other citrus fruits, such as Clementines and Satsumas. I have had personal dealings with both these citrus fruit trees and recommend them as suitable species for beginner citrus container gardeners to try out.

Clementines

If you want to enjoy deliciously sweet Mandarins but don't want to wait 4 – 7 years for your first harvest, Clementines are a great choice as they produce their first crop within the first year.

Clementines are an exciting fruit tree because they are a hybrid of the Sweet Orange and Willowleaf Mandarin Orange and have a high pest resistance. They are also highly ornamental with their round ever-green canopy of leaves and fragrant white blossoms (spring).

Clementines have a deep orange color and a smooth skin that's thin and easy to peel with a sweet 7 – 14 segment interior. While Clementines originate from China, they were first "discovered" by the western world in an orphanage garden in Misserghin in French Algeria.

Most of the world's Clementine production happens in China, but it may be of interest to you that areas such as California, Spain, and Morocco have earned quite a reputation for growing them too.

Something unique about growing Clementine trees is they have lower heat requirements than other citrus trees, making them less sensitive to low temperatures. If you grow Clementines in high-heat areas, they usually bear fruit earlier than expected. The tree itself is thorny, so be prepared to use gloves when working with it.

Satsuma

The Satsuma is a seedless Mandarin often chosen as the ideal citrus container gardening species for its easy-peeling leathery skin and the fact that it's one of the sweetest citrus varieties around. Each fruit features 10 – 12 segments with tough membranes that are easy to separate. The flesh is reddish-orange and delicate, so it cannot withstand mishandling.

Satsumas are also ornamental with dark-colored green leaves and bright white blossoms when in bloom.

One of the most interesting titbits of information about Satsumas is that the colder their environment is, the sweeter the fruit will be. They are even able to withstand temperatures as low as 12 degrees Fahrenheit (-11 degrees Celsius)!

When grown from seed, it can take between 4 and 8 years to produce fruit. Another alternative is to buy it in rootstock form to speed up the fruit production. Satsuma trees originated from China and arrived in the Western world via Japan. Nowadays, the tree is popularly grown in Spain, Japan, China, the USA, South Africa, Korea, South America, New Zealand, and even in the UK (as garden plants or container plants).

Mandarin Tree Pests & Diseases

Like other citrus fruit trees, pests and diseases target the Mandarin tree. Being prepared for the risks will enable you to protect your tree from possible infestations and infections. The most common Mandarin tree pests and diseases are listed below, but more in-depth information on identification (symptoms), preventative measures, and treatments are in Chapter Six.

Pests that Target Mandarin Trees

- Aphids
- Leaf Miners
- Soft Scales
- Thrips

Diseases that Target Mandarin Trees

- Anthracnose
- Armillaria Root Rot
- Black Root Rot
- Blast
- Brown Rot
- Citrus Canker
- Tristeza Disease

2

SELECTING THE CORRECT CONTAINER OR POT

Growing citrus fruit trees can be a complicated process if you're unfamiliar with them. Like all of us, fruit trees have their lifestyle preferences. They like what they like, and if you're willing to attune yourself to their needs and "wants", you will grow trees that produce and thrive.

First and foremost, it's essential to know that citrus trees can be pretty sensitive to weather conditions. They also have specific soil requirements and need a considerable amount of care. The perceived amount of effort can be off-putting to many gardeners.

That said, growing citrus fruit trees in *containers* is an entirely different story.

Choosing to plant and grow your trees in containers instead of directly in the ground gives you the upper hand. Half the proverbial battle is already won. For starters, you will have the flexibility to move your trees around to find out where they genuinely thrive.

Keeping your trees indoors also provides an added layer of protection against pests and diseases. Containers also allow you to overcome poor soil conditions without having to put in too much effort or fork out a hefty amount of money.

Lastly, the beauty of container gardening is that you get to give your fruit trees the best of both worlds. You can shift them indoors and outdoors with the changing seasons, protecting them from the elements as needed. As such, container gardening allows you to provide your fruit trees with the best possible chance of survival.

It's safe to say that one of the most important decisions you will make when growing citrus fruit trees in containers is choosing which pot or container you will use. Most people don't know this, but the container can either boost or thwart your fruit tree's growth.

It's important to know what a citrus fruit tree likes and dislikes, which will help you choose pots and containers that fit the purpose. Before you can get stuck into container gardening, you have to select the correct containers for the trees you will be growing, so let's talk pots and containers.

For citrus fruit trees, you need a pot that doesn't trap too much heat if it's left in the sun. You also need the container to hold a decent amount of water without becoming water-logged.

Finding containers with good drainage should be on the top of your list of priorities.

While selecting your pots, keep your specific climate in mind. If the pot/container remains outdoors, you need to consider how cold or hot it might get. In some instances, pots can crack when they get too cold. On the flip side, some containers can cook your plant's roots if they trap heat on a hot day.

Container gardening indoors allows you to provide the ideal growing conditions for your trees with no worries about being too hot or too cold.

The first step is to consider the various types of pots and containers available.

TYPES OF CONTAINERS & POTS TO CHOOSE FROM

You can choose pots that are fun and fit in with your current décor, but they should be functional too. Consider how each container will impact your plant's growth and whether you are making a sound, long-term investment. You will find three main *types* of pots/containers: non-porous, semi-porous, and porous.

Below we investigate each type of pot/container.

Non-Porous Pots and Containers

Metal, plastic, fiberglass glazed, and ceramic containers are all considered non-porous. One of the main benefits of non-porous pots is that they offer excellent water retention. If you don't have a lot of free time available to tend to your trees, you might find this helpful because your trees won't need watering as often as if you use semi-porous or porous pots.

One thing to be aware of is the difficulty of gardening with black plastic pots and containers, especially if your trees will be standing in the sun. Black plastic pots tend to trap heat. Over time, the trapped heat can cook the roots of your tree and dry out the soil quickly. A fruit tree with cooked roots will start to wither and die, much like a constantly thirsty fruit tree.

Semi-Porous Pots and Containers

An excellent example of a semi-porous container is one made out of wood. The natural appeal of wood looks good in outdoor and indoor settings, making wooden containers the first choice for many.

When cold or hot weather strikes, wood stands up to the challenge; it doesn't crack in the cold and is slow to dry out in the heat. One of the biggest problems that gardeners face with wooden pots and containers is the risk of rot setting in. You can line the planter with plastic and treat the exterior of the wood to provide better protection. However, lining the pot could negatively impact drainage, so it's a good idea to investigate your options wisely when considering a semi-porous wooden container.

Some tips for using wooden planters include:

- Apply roofing cement to the inside of the wooden planter to protect it from water damage and rot
- Use landscape fabric to layer the bottom of the container to deter the soil from washing out through the drainage holes and plank cracks/gaps
- Only use high-quality well-draining soil to avoid waterlogging

Porous Pots and Containers

Some fine examples of porous pots and containers are the clay, unglazed ceramic, mesh/fabric, and terracotta pots available on the market. Porous containers don't offer a lot of water retention, so they're great for trees that need good drainage.

Porous pots and containers can help with citrus tree container gardening, but you should probably avoid using unglazed ceramic pots if your trees remain outdoors. This is because these pots tend to hold a lot of moisture, and when the temperature drops, the pot may end up freezing or cracking. Both of these outcomes aren't pleasant for a citrus tree.

Signs of a Decent Pot

Whether you opt for a porous, semi-porous, or non-porous pot, the simple fact is that you need to ensure it's a good fit for your environment and your citrus tree. Ensure that your chosen containers and pots offer the following conveniences:

Sufficient drainage holes

All citrus fruit trees dislike being waterlogged and prefer decent root aeration. Because of this, your pots and containers need multiple drainage holes. You may find that most containers only have one central drainage hole, usually located in the middle of the container's base. If the pot only has one drainage hole but is otherwise a good pot, it doesn't have to be excluded as a viable option. You can simply drill a few additional holes into the container (4 – 6 evenly-spaced holes are sufficient).

Standing feet

By now, you have probably noticed that most gardening pots come with drainage trays, aka drip trays. While these have their purpose, they aren't entirely practical if you will be moving your containers between an indoor and outdoor space. Also, the trays trap excess drained water. Two things can happen if your citrus tree is standing in water all day; the roots become soggy and start to rot and, mosquitos find it a pleasant place to breed.

It's a far better idea to look for pots and containers with feet or built-in casters (these are wheels). Alternatively, get rid of the drip tray and invest in a caddy that will at least help you move your tree around when the weather starts to change.

CONSIDER THE WEIGHT OF POTS & CONTAINERS

I learned the hard way that someone isn't always going to be around to help with the heavy lifting when you're tending to your citrus fruit trees. You might have grand ideas of a picturesque fruit tree garden complete with ornate pots, but those dreams are dashed when you're trying to lug and heave the tree and pot around singlehandedly.

Just think of how heavy a 6ft tall (1.8m) citrus tree with soil in a pot is. Basically, before you commit to buying a pot, consider how heavy it will be when there's a tree planted in it.

To help you choose the correct container with weight in mind, here's what you need to know:

Plastic Pots

As far as container weights go, plastic pots are the lightest and easiest to move around. You must be careful when selecting a plastic pot, though. Ensure that the plastic is of decent quality, or you may find that the pot breaks when you try to move the tree around.

You also need to consider the type and size of the citrus tree you have in mind. Some citrus trees are more prolific producers than others which could make them top-heavy in a lightweight pot. Much the same, citrus trees with big heavy fruit could cause a top-heavy effect too.

Using a container that's *too* light could result in the tree toppling over unexpectedly or when a slight breeze comes up (when the tree is outside).

Terracotta Pots

Terracotta pots and containers are top choices for many people because of their aesthetic appeal. Unfortunately, while terracotta pots are good-looking, they can be a struggle to move around. These pots are quite heavy even when they are empty.

These are porous pots, which means you need to water your tree regularly, adding to the weight. They won't make moving your tree from one spot to another or between indoor and outdoor spaces very easy.

Fabric and Cloth Pots

If you're focused on environmentally friendly options, fabric and cloth pots are a great choice. Their reusability is low, but they have less of an environmental impact than other pot types. What's great about fabric and cloth pots is that they help citrus trees develop strong and fibrous roots, which goes a long way towards reducing the need for pruning and keeping them healthy.

As far as weight is concerned, a cloth pot is almost weightless, so you're just working with the weight of the tree and the soil when you move things around.

SELECTING A SUITABLE CONTAINER COLOR

You may think that the color of your citrus tree's container is irrelevant, but that's incorrect. The color of a plant's container plays a considerable role in whether it lives and thrives or withers and dies.

As you learn more about citrus fruit trees, you will discover that they enjoy having moderately cool roots. As soon as their roots are hot or bake (or boil) for a considerable amount of time, they stop thriving. Because of this, the color of the pots you choose is essential.

Opt for light colors or natural colors such as green, tan, sandy brown, white, or similar. Avoid dark colors as they tend to absorb and trap the sun's heat, which can niggle the tree roots when they get hot.

SELECTING THE CORRECT CONTAINER SHAPE AND SIZE

Many first-time citrus gardeners overlook the importance of the container's shape and size. The pot's shape will affect how sturdy the tree is as it grows and determine how the excess water drains from the pot. For instance, a container with a narrow base/stand that has a heavy citrus tree in it will not stand firm forever. At some point, it is going to become top-heavy and topple over.

It is essential to choose a pot with a broad, sturdy base to support the tree's weight, especially when moved around. On the flip side, a container with a very narrow mouth will also be awkward to work with, especially when repotting trees (the roots may not come out of the container), so choose something with a suitable entry point.

One reason for choosing a pot of the right size is that root restriction can slow down your tree's growth and lead to poor-quality fruit production. Stress inflicted on a fruit tree's roots can cause root surface damage, prime for plant diseases and infestations.

Citrus fruit trees are steady growers, and they respond best when you're willing to grow with them. That means that you need to be aware of their growth speed and have the next pot ready to transfer it to when it reaches a bigger size. You have to increase the size of the container as the tree grows.

When you first start citrus container gardening, you can get away with a young plant in an 8in (20cm) diameter container. Your citrus tree will be pretty happy with that for at least the first 1 – 2 years unless your tree is a fast grower!

Top tip: *do not start with a large container in hopes that your tree will "grow into it". Unfortunately, this is not how it works with citrus trees. You will find that it becomes difficult to control the soil's moisture levels for such a small tree in such an oversized pot. In the end, you will negatively impact the tree's growth.*

Note: The only instance where it is good to plant a citrus tree straight into a very large container is if you're working with micro-budded citrus trees. A micro-budded citrus tree is a tree that is grafted, which usually spurs rapid growth of the tree and root system.

Because a micro-budded citrus tree has a different way of growing from regular citrus trees, it is acceptable to plant it directly into a 16 – 20-gallon container. This ensures that the roots don't bunch too soon and that your water drainage doesn't become compromised.

If you're growing a regular citrus tree, instead of rushing the process by selecting a bigger pot than required, prepare to go through the growing process with your trees by sizing up pots as needed. It's best to increase pot size by pot size to ensure the tree remains comfortable at every stage of growth.

You need a pot with a 10 – 12in (25 – 30cm) diameter for smaller trees – this is typically called a "five-gallon container" at most nurseries, which is fine for the first 2 – 3 years.

Mature trees (older than three years) need 16 – 20-gallon containers at least 18 –24in (45 – 60cm) deep. This will give your citrus tree's roots plenty of room to grow and ensure the pot doesn't become top-heavy and topple over.

A quick size guide for containers:

Citrus plant size/stage	Container size
Germinated seed (1.5in/4cm roots)	3in (1cm) diameter and at least 5in (2cm) tall
Seedling citrus tree in its first year	28in (71cm) diameter pot
2 – 3-year-old citrus tree	16 – 20 gallon container, 18 – 24in (45 –63cm) deep

Repotting

All citrus trees need to be repotted from time to time. This is not only because of aesthetics but also to refresh the soil, inspect the roots (they may need trimming), and give your tree a fresh, new environment to thrive. After all, they do say that change is as good as a holiday. Who doesn't thrive after a holiday?!

3

PLANTING CITRUS TREES

Much like humans, citrus trees are sensitive to their surroundings. They like what they like, and if you don't make them comfortable, they're going to experience a level of discomfort/unhappiness that soon becomes evident. That said, every citrus tree needs a good foundation, and you can provide that for your trees by ensuring that you plant them correctly the first time around. Planting a citrus tree involves more forethought and preparation than simply popping a tree into a pot with some soil. The planting process requires a few steps described below:

- Get to know what your citrus tree likes and dislikes

- Select the correct pot (we covered this in Chapter Two)
- Prepare the soil to ensure it's in line with what your citrus tree likes
- Position the tree in the correct place for its light and temperature needs

The good news is that it doesn't matter which of our selected citrus trees you choose to grow; the planting instructions for each are the same. It's pretty convenient if you have decided to produce a selection of citrus trees because they all seem to have similar planting requirements.

This chapter focuses on all the ins and outs you need to know about preparing and planting your citrus tree. Included in this chapter also is information on planting depth and using the correct soil mix.

The featured planting instructions cover the following citrus trees:

- Kumquats
- Lemons
- Limes
- Oranges
- Mandarins

GERMINATING CITRUS SEEDS

Before we look at preparing soil mixes to plant citrus seedlings and trees, let's consider that you may want to grow your citrus tree from seed yourself. If this is the case, you will need to germinate your citrus seeds before planting them into small pots or seedling trays. There are two main ways of sprouting citrus trees: in a paper towel or soil. Below are some general directions for germinating citrus seeds using both these methods:

Germinating citrus seeds: **the paper towel method**

1. Remove seeds from the desired fruit – choose the biggest and healthiest looking seeds from the batch.
2. Using warm water (not hot), rinse the seeds and dry them.
3. Gently peel off the outer skin of the seed. This is an optional step, but your seeds will sprout faster if you do this.
4. You can further speed up the sprouting process by soaking them in lukewarm water overnight.
5. Wrap the seeds into a warm paper towel and place them inside a plastic bag which should then be sealed. Make a note of the date on the bag using a marker.
6. Place the bag in a warm shaded spot (no light is required) – under the kitchen sink is a good option.
7. Check on the seeds regularly to ensure that the bag is still moist inside.
8. After 10 – 14 days, the seeds should have healthy roots developing and are ready for planting.

Germinating citrus seeds: **directly into the soil**

1. Fill a container with potting soil, leaving a 1in (3cm) gap between the soil and the container's top lip.
2. Pick seeds out of your chosen citrus fruit and rinse them with warm water.
3. Push each seed about 0.3 inches (1cm) deep into the soil, cover up with soil and water.
4. Place the container inside a plastic bag (use an elastic

band to keep the bag in place) and then poke a few holes into the bag to allow air to pass through.

5. Place the container in a warm spot (not too warm) and wait for 10-14 days. The seeds should sprout within this time.

PREPARING CITRUS FRUIT TREE SOIL MIX FOR CONTAINER GARDENING

Citrus container gardening isn't complicated, but it does require you to pay attention, learn what your trees need, and be meticulous and consistent about caring for them. Just like raising children, you need to have your citrus trees in mind every day. Even if it's only to check on them for pests and disease or do soil moisture checks, be prepared to spend time with your trees daily.

For this reason, I feel it is crucial to spend some time focusing on what sort of soil mix citrus trees like when being potted. It's also vital that you gather information on preparing your soil to please your chosen citrus trees in the days ahead.

Here's the reality: when choosing to do container gardening, you become the sole controller of all the soil, nutrients, and water your citrus tree gets. No pressure, but that's quite a responsibility. The soil mix you choose and how you go about planting your citrus tree impacts its life.

A bump in the tree's road could lead to long-term problems that are hard to overcome, so the most effective thing to do is to aim for prevention instead of cure. Many people who are new to gardening overlook the importance of a nutritious citrus-friendly soil mix. Unfortunately, neglecting the soil mix could end in the ultimate demise of your citrus tree.

Citrus trees have specific soil preferences, and if you don't cater to their needs and wants, they will start to show their discontent in the form of:

- Inadequate fruit production
- Stunted growth
- Withering and dying

It can be pretty disheartening to fail so early on in the process, so treat soil like a number one commodity in your citrus tree's life. Soil is life for a citrus tree, so try to give your tree the best life possible!

AVOID USING SOIL FROM YOUR GARDEN

One of the first things I learned as a newbie to the container gardening world is that if you want to ensure that your citrus trees thrive, avoid using soil directly from your garden. You may look around you and think how convenient it is to have so much ground readily at your disposal, but it's a better choice to choose a soil mix or potting soil. Here's why:

- Soil mixes contain ingredients that make the soil less compactible. Soil mix makes it easier for the citrus tree to manage life in a container
- Soil mixes include ingredients for aeration, drainage, and nutrients. These ingredients can cater to the specific needs of your tree
- With garden soil, it is a hit-and-miss situation. Your soil could have a spider mite infestation or another type of infection with which you can infest your tree

If you must use soil from your garden, make sure to spend some time modifying it before you introduce it to your tree. Sometimes a soil mix that isn't suited to a citrus tree can be modified to better suit it by adding a few ingredients. It just requires a little know-how.

The big question is: "what do citrus trees like in a soil mix?" Citrus trees like lightweight, high porosity soil mix – it's that simple.

Many beginners make the mistake of over-complicating it when it comes to the soil mix. It's not anyone's fault. Most people assume they know more about growing citrus and other trees than they do. Some beginners fall into the trap of listening to nursery staff members' generic advice because they may not know better.

Some may take guidance from friends on what they believe "citrus trees love" and become disappointed when their trees don't respond as anticipated. I am here to say it loud and clear; keep it as simple as possible when preparing the soil for your tree and planting it.

Give your citrus trees what they want. Don't go above and beyond by adding, feeding, and fertilizing in excess. You may end up disappointed when your trees decide that they don't like it at all.

Naturally, you can't go wrong if you buy a commercial potting mix specifically advertised for citrus trees, but this isn't always available. If that's the case, you may find yourself standing at the nursery with a plethora of options to choose from and not the faintest idea of what to do. Having at least *some* understanding of soil mixes will help you understand what products are out there and what you can do to make the standard options even better.

AMENDING SOIL MIXES

A lot of newbie gardeners think that soil mixes are all the same. Even if the soil mix doesn't seem ideal for the plant, they may go ahead and try it out anyway. You could take your chances, but rather don't. It's not that you have to spend a lot of money on the soil. It's not about brand names and expensive additives. It's just about making a wise decision for your plant. The soil mix that you use is a type of investment in your tree's longevity and productivity.

Always approach a nursery visit with an open mind. Remember that you can alter many of the products on offer to suit your tree's needs by adding other soil types or organic matter.

I have learned along the way that you don't have to buy an expensive soil mix if you want the "good stuff". Instead, create your soil mix based on your knowledge of your trees. Take the time to study what the soil mix consists of before you commit to it. If it's not quite what citrus trees want, you can make alterations in the following ways. Here's what to do in the following scenarios:

The soil mix has a high content of dense and absorbent material.

If you can only find a soil mix with a lot of absorbent and dense material in it, potting your citrus trees with it isn't going to work. By now, you already know that citrus trees like lightweight, well-draining soil. Because of this, you need to provide your tree with precisely that.

I know that you will probably come across many soil mixes that include peat moss and worm castings from personal experience. I often shy away from these because they can be pretty dense and absorbent, which traps water. Remember that your citrus trees like water, but they don't want to be trapped in it. Soil that traps moisture goes against the drainage needs of a citrus tree, of course.

In my experience, not all citrus trees will tolerate poor drainage, especially if it's a long-term thing. It doesn't specifically mean that all hope is lost if soil mix with dense and absorbent materials is all that's available, though. Altering it can make it far more appealing to the average citrus tree – here's how to do that.

To alter the soil, add ¼ – 1/3 volume of 1in Redwood shavings (Cedar shavings work just as well) and mix in well.

The soil mix is heavy

Of course, you know that citrus trees like high-porosity soil mix, so if all you can find is a heavy soil mix, you're going to have to modify the soil. Unfortunately, high porosity soil mix isn't the easiest thing to find.

Historically, one solution to heavy soils has been to add wood-chips, and specifically hardwood chips. Many nurseries still do this today, but it is not a long-term solution, but rather a means of making a quick mix for growth, sale, and transport, with the assumption that the grower will repot the plant into a more appropriate final mix.

Similarly, many nurseries will add woodshavings to their mix as a loose filler; but, again, this is not intended for long-term plantings. Woodshavings and interior sapwood should be avoided because they decompose rapidly, which leads to soil collapse and compaction, and ultimately suffocation of the roots. Additionally, Cedar shavings may contain allelopathic chemicals that could deter or inhibit root growth, making it more difficult for the plant to establish roots in the new potting mix.

When using hardwood chips, microbes break down the wood, leading to nitrogen binding and nitrogen immobilization. This is when the microbes in the soil compete with the plant for nutrients. Nitrogen immobilization leads to soil organisms taking up the nitrate and ammonium in the soil and leaving little for the tree.

Pine and Spruce shavings aren't nearly as long-lasting, so avoid opting for these.

To amend heavy soil, add a bit of water to the mix to make it easy to work with, and then adjust it by adding 1/3 – ½ of the volume of 1in shavings. In this format, the soil is ready and fit for a citrus tree.

The soil mix includes chemical wetting agents and fertilizers

You may notice that some soil mixes, especially those sold for indoor use, include fertilizers and chemical wetting agents. While it may seem like a sound idea to buy one of these, it often hinders the tree's progress, so it's better to avoid them.

Why don't citrus trees like chemical wetting agents and fertilizers? It's all about citrus tree preferences. Chemical wetting agents usually keep the tree's roots wet for too long, and the fertilizer included may burn the tree's roots. All in all, it's not the best idea to invest in one of these soil mixes for your citrus trees.

SHOULD YOU FERTILIZE WHEN PREPARING PLANTING SOIL MIX?

Many people wrongly believe that fertilizer is the most critical factor when it comes to preparing soil mix. The truth is that you need to go easy with fertilizer on a citrus tree, especially when re-potting or planting for the first time. Avoid using fertilizer straight away, as this can cause the roots to burn.

Keep in mind that when the tree's roots are tampered with, even just for re-potting, it can impact the tree. If you want to add to the mix, opt for Vitamin B1 rooting tonic and only add a slow-release fertilizer to the soil's surface once the re-potted tree's roots have settled into their new home.

Give your tree a bit of time; otherwise, it may begin to feel a little overwhelmed or bombarded. When citrus tree gardening in containers, you have far more control over the soil, but that also means that you have the potential to overdo it.

PREPARING THE IDEAL CITRUS SOIL MIX

Preparing a soil mix for citrus trees doesn't have to be complicated. For best results, merely keep it simple. There are plenty of expensive products on the market, but you don't need them specifically. Of course, you are free to buy and use them if you want to.

The trick to creating a citrus-friendly soil mix is to start with decent rich organic soil. If you have that, you are onto a good thing as your base is ready. If you want to bulk up a potting soil mix, you need to consider organic fillers. Fillers don't just bulk up the potting soil; they enhance the soil's structure, durability, and drainage. Another benefit of using organic fillers is that it improves aeration, nutrient retention and ensures that the soil maintains the appropriate moisture levels.

So, what makes for a good organic filler for container citrus trees? In my opinion, that would be the outer bark from Hemlock, Pine, Fir, and Spruce. The reason why I like these conifer barks, in particular, is that they are rich in Lignin and Suberin, which delays decay and microbial breakdown. The pieces of bark are ideal at around ¼ inch – ½ inch – any bigger, and they will deter good drainage and prove quite challenging to work with.

If you want to create a potting soil mix that is highly durable and porous, too, you should start with 50% bark. You can also use coconut husk chips and amending the soil with the likes of lava rock, pumice, and Perlite. I have found that horticultural charcoal is also quite effective.

PLANTING CITRUS TREES AT THE CORRECT DEPTH

If you plant your citrus tree at the wrong depth, it may negatively impact the tree's life expectancy. Most of the tree's roots will be at the surface – at the first 18 inches (45cm) of soil. If you plant it too shallow, it could result in exposed roots or the tree becoming top-heavy and pulling out of the soil as it falls over or to the side.

If you plant it too deeply, you may make it difficult for the tree's roots to have space to expand.

How you plant your citrus tree will depend on whether you have a nursery-bought grafted tree (rootstock), a mail-order tree (usually arrives in shavings), or a tree you have grown from seedling and are re-potting.

While the planting process is the same, the difference comes in with nursery-bought trees. These trees must be removed from the bag and planted at the same level. The grafting scar (called the graft union) should be positioned just above the soil level when planted into the pot/container.

10 STEPS FOR PLANTING OR RE-POTTING A CITRUS TREE

1. First, prepare the soil mix so that it is suitable for a citrus tree.
2. Place the soil mix into your chosen container. Only fill the container up to the point where, if your tree rested on top of it, the roots would be below the soil's surface line when the pot is full of dirt. Never place the tree's roots on the container's base and fill it up with soil as you will be planting your tree too deep for root expansion and healthy growth.
3. Remove the citrus tree from the old container. Ensure that you take exceptional care when removing the tree from an old container. It may seem like your citrus tree is hardy, but often damage happens during potting or re-potting. Be careful to slide the roots out without allowing any damage. If you remove a citrus tree from a black nursery bag, cut the bag off so that you don't damage the tree in the process of getting it out. Often the roots can get stuck or grow through the drainage holes, so go as slowly as you can.
4. Before you pot the tree, you need to work on it. Place the tree onto a flat surface (the grass or a table is fine) and spend some time trimming off dead roots. Focus on detangling any roots that have circled the old container. The roots may have become compacted or root bound, especially if the tree has been in the container for an extended time. Again, when dealing with the roots, handle with care as excess damage can upset the tree. Detangling and trimming ensure healthy root growth in the new pot.
5. It's time to add your fruit tree to the container in which

it will live out its life (until the next re-potting, that is). Now that the root ball is loosened and free from dead roots, gently place it onto the soil mix in the container. Without pushing the tree down, ensure the tree is in the center of the pot. Check that the roots will only be slightly below the surface when you eventually fill the container with soil mix.

6. Carefully fill the container up with the rest of your soil mix. Try using a small spade or a scoop to add soil so that you can shuffle the soil around the tree evenly without knocking it or potentially damaging it.

7. Pack the soil down gently, but don't push too hard. Citrus trees aren't fans of overly compacted soil, so only light pressing is required. You want to push out any large air pockets.

8. Examine the re-potted tree to ensure that it's suitably potted. The citrus tree's roots should be just covered and with no soil packed up against the tree's trunk. The tree should also be standing straight and able to support itself (by being planted at the correct depth and position).

9. Thoroughly water the container. The soil should be completely soaked, and it should drain out quickly. Pay attention to this because if the soil mix isn't quite right, it won't drain efficiently. If you find that the soil sinks right down when you water it, don't worry - add a bit more soil mix to compensate for the shrinkage.

10. Repeat this re-potting process every 1 – 2 years (3 – 4 years at a push) to ensure the happiness and longevity of your citrus trees. You know it's time to re-pot the tree when the roots start to find their way through their drainage holes below.

Now that you know everything you need to know about preparing the soil mix and potting (and re-potting) your citrus tree, it's time to move on to learning about *caring* for your citrus trees.

In the next chapter, we take a look at general tips for potted citrus trees.

4

GENERAL TIPS FOR POTTED CITRUS TREES

Taking care of a citrus tree isn't difficult but takes meticulous work. You cannot plant a citrus tree and expect it to care for itself. Citrus trees have particular requirements in terms of watering and drainage, temperature, fertilizer and compost, light, positioning, pests, and more.

Having a general understanding of your tree's needs and what to do when problems arise will ensure that your citrus container gardening experience is a simplified and rewarding one. The sections below cover everything you need to know about the average citrus tree's wants and needs. Keep these in mind when tending to your trees.

GOOD DRAINAGE

Poor drainage means certain death for citrus trees. They are pretty particular about this need. I would go as far as to say that this point is "non-negotiable".

Symptoms of poor drainage:

- Yellowing leaves
- Drooping leaves
- Leaf drop
- Constantly damp soil
- Presence of Fungus Gnats

When working with citrus trees, you need to ensure that the drainage you provide is nothing short of excellent. A citrus tree left standing in a soggy pot will wither and die. When you water the tree, it should flow right through the container and out through the drainage holes. There should be absolutely no waterlogging to any degree.

This is where soil mixes with shredded hardwood are pretty helpful because they allow the water to pass right through them without disintegrating, whereas softer wood such as pine tends to disintegrate far too quickly.

We have already covered how to prepare your soil mix, so pay special attention to this when planting your citrus tree. If you have the right soil mix and your container has enough drainage holes below, you should have adequate drainage.

If you're growing your citrus tree in a closed or ornamental pot, you need to be moderate with how much water your pour into the pot. If, for some reason, the tree does end up standing in water (perhaps someone overwaters the tree by accident, or it is left standing outside), do not let the tree remain standing in the water for more than 12 hours.

MOISTURE AND MOISTURE METER

A moisture meter is a citrus tree owner's best friend! Citrus trees need moisture but don't like it *too much*, making moisture control a tricky balancing act. The watering needs of citrus trees in pots are different from citrus trees planted directly in the ground. This is because the roots are contained and can dry out quickly or be trapped in water. By investing in a moisture meter, there's no umming and ahhing over the amount of moisture your tree's soil has. You can keep the levels constantly monitored and adjust as required.

To use one of these devices, insert the meter into the soil mix and let it do its job. If you're working with a citrus tree in a huge pot, take several readings before you settle on a final one. When you water your citrus tree, the meter should read a level 10. You don't need to water the tree again until the meter reading drops to a level of 2 – 3.

WATERING, OVER-WATERING & UNDER-WATERING

You may think that you are doing your citrus trees a favor by topping them up with water every day, but the reality is that over-watering citrus trees can result in death. Many people overlook this fact so much that over-watering is the number one cause of citrus trees dying.

The fact that citrus trees don't like to be over-watered doesn't mean that you should "sip water" your tree. Citrus trees also have a bad reaction to being under-watered. Essentially, it means that when you water the tree, drench the soil thoroughly, but only water it again when the soil has almost completely dried out.

Symptoms of over-watering:

- Drooping leaves (not dried out, though)
- Yellowing leaves
- Dropping leaves
- Presence of Fungus Gnats

Symptoms of under-watering:

- Soil pulls away from the sides of the pot
- Water pools on top of the soil before soaking in
- Water quickly pours through the soil as if none is absorbed
- Dropping leaves
- Dry or crispy leaves
- Dried out branches in sections

Terracotta pots can help you avoid overwatering because they leave a dark/damp tell-tale mark on the pot's base (outside) when there's still water in the soil. Even if the top of the soil looks and feels dry, but you are aware that there is water in the bottom of the pot, don't water the tree. Wait.

If you aren't using a terracotta pot and prefer to use a touch-and-feel method of telling when your tree needs water, when the top of the soil looks dry, give it a feel. If the top 2in (5cm) of soil are dry, it's time to rewater your tree.

To ensure that you never over-water or under-water your plant, it is a good idea to develop a watering schedule. To do this, you first need to do a bit of investigative work. Once your tree is potted and positioned, drench the soil and monitor how long it takes for the pot to almost dry out. Then repeat the exercise.

After doing this 2 – 3 times, you should have an idea of your tree's watering schedule. Pop a reminder on your fridge or set a calendar event/alarm on your mobile phone so that you never miss watering day.

THE TEMPERATURE OF WATER USED

Just like you don't like jumping into an ice-cold bath of water, citrus trees don't like cold water poured onto their roots. In fact, they detest cold water, which should come as no surprise as most tropical and subtropical trees are designed for warm climates.

Symptoms of using water that's too cold:

- Yellowing leaf veins
- Dropping leaves

Ensure that you provide your citrus tree with tepid or room-temperature water. If you're using a watering can, you can add some hot water to cold tap water to increase the water temperature.

USE OF FERTILIZER

Citrus trees are hungry plants. Some like to call them "heavy feeders" because of their desire for food. Of course, they're not hungry for just anything – they want nitrogen. When fertilizing, it is vital that you use the correct quantity of nitrogen fertilizer and don't go overboard.

Symptoms of over-fertilizing:

- Yellowing leaves
- Wilting leaves
- Brown roots
- Rotting roots
- Browning leaf margins (tips and edges)
- Dropping leaves
- Stunted growth

If you were growing citrus trees outside, you would find that they feed less during winter when planted directly in the soil. Indoor container citrus plants do not slow down during winter, so you will need to maintain your fertilizing schedule. Your citrus tree thinks that it's summer still, and it will grow and thrive (and feed) throughout the season.

If you haven't been fertilizing your plants, it's undoubtedly time to start when you see flowers and tiny fruits appearing. The tree will need sufficient nutrition to grow the fruit to full maturity.

You need to develop a fertilizing schedule because well-draining soil and a healthy watering schedule will lead to nutrients washing out. It would help if you fertilized the tree at least once a month, but I usually fertilize lightly every two weeks to aid as the trees go through different growth phases. You can get pellet nitrogen fertilizer, but seaweed and fish fertilizers work just as well if you're willing to deal with the smell. Don't worry; it goes away in a day or two.

It's important to note that fertilizer sticks are not ideal for citrus trees grown in pots. They may seem convenient, but they can burn the roots of the tree, so always opt for an organic fertilizer if you want to avoid that risk. Of course, you should always follow the instructions on the fertilizer packaging.

USE OF COMPOST & CITRUS PH REQUIREMENTS

Using compost in your citrus tree's soil mix can be highly beneficial to its growth because the roots can spread with ease, and there's the provision of a nutrient-dense growing environment. Of course, you have to use the proper compost for your citrus tree. Don't opt for general-purpose composts because they contain lime, which increases the soil's pH level (something a citrus tree does *not* like).

The pH level of your citrus tree's soil will impact how it absorbs nutrients and minerals in the soil. The fruit yield of a citrus tree is greatly improved when the soil's pH level is low, which allows the plant to better absorb calcium, zinc, iron, manganese, and phosphorus. The ideal pH of soil for citrus trees is between 6.0 – 6.5. Don't attempt to take your citrus tree's soil pH any lower, as anything below 5.0 is toxic to a citrus tree.

When choosing compost for citrus trees, opt for ericaceous compost, which is ideal for lime-hating plants.

LIGHT REQUIREMENTS

It goes without saying that citrus trees thoroughly enjoy the sunlight. Full sunlight will make your citrus tree happy, but you must move your potted tree indoors when the temperatures start to drop. It's important to know that a citrus tree likes at least 6 – 8 hours of sunlight a day, but this doesn't mean that there's no such thing as *too much* sunlight in a citrus tree's life. When exposed to too much light, say 12 hours a day, citrus trees go into a vegetative state. They become stressed and sleep-deprived, which leads to poor or halted fruit production.

Symptoms of insufficient sunlight:

- Leaves dropping
- Burnt leaves
- Poor growth

Symptoms of too much sunlight:

- Wilting leaves
- Poor quality fruit or no fruit at all

You can provide your citrus tree with light in two main ways mentioned below:

Indirect Sunlight Through Windows

Choose a sunny room or build a structure in a bright spot for citrus trees. Place the pots close to the windows so that they get to enjoy the sunlight streaming in. Choose your tree's dedicated window or light source with care.

Artificial Sunlight with Lighting

If you buy lights to help grow your citrus trees indoors, make sure that you don't expose your trees to too much light. Increasing light exposure will not increase fruit production. A citrus tree needs no more than 8 hours of sunlight per day. This is because the tree follows a particular flowering and fruiting schedule. Exposing the tree to too much light can throw this schedule off and actually result in little or no fruit production.

When it comes to artificial lighting, keep in mind that citrus trees have different light intensity requirements from other vegetables and herbs. You will find many lights available on the market made from plastic and metal. I feel that ceramic lighting is a better option because they provide ample lighting while conserving energy (great for the eco-friendly at heart).

Opt for full-spectrum lighting that you can adjust to your needs. 24W LED full-spectrum lighting is specifically helpful because it imitates UV lighting more accurately than other types of lights. These lights offer a mix of the light spectrum for growth, leaf flush, blossoming, and fruiting. You can set this kind of light 6 – 18 inches (15 – 45cm) away from your tree and expect to use one light for 1 – 3 trees.

Moving Plants Back Outside After Winter

A citrus tree has no place outside during the cold winters. If you're growing fruit trees in containers, you have the convenience of being able to bring the trees indoors when winter comes around. Citrus fruit trees freeze at temperatures that drop to 26 –28 degrees Fahrenheit (-2 degrees Celsius). As you can imagine, this isn't going to bode well for a sunlight-loving tree.

When you move your citrus trees indoors in the cooler months, you will need to have a strategy for moving them back out again when the warmer months come around. Keep in mind that your citrus plant has been indoors for quite some time and is not used to the full might of sunshine on it. Be gradual about returning your trees to full sunlight.

First, move your citrus trees into a spot that offers dappled sunlight. Allow them to grow in this space for 2 – 3 weeks before moving them into full sun. You need to follow the same process (in reverse) when moving your trees back indoors when the cooler months come around again.

As a point of interest and a top tip for new container gardeners, small, young plants should not be moved outside during their first season of growth. Protect the tree and improve its chance of survival by keeping it indoors for the first season.

DRAFTS & RADIATORS

Citrus trees aren't fans of drafts or radiator blasts, so it's best to protect them from these. Air stress can cause a healthy tree to develop unexpected growth issues. If you think it is a good idea to open a window near the tree to "give them a bit of air", rather don't. The cold air will unsettle your tree and stress it, which will leave them more susceptible to disease and pests too.

Symptoms of air stress:

- Brown leaf edges
- Leaves dropping
- Fruit dropping

The excess heat from a radiator or underfloor heating can also stress a citrus tree, so position your trees away from heat sources. While you are keeping your trees indoors to protect them from the cold, you shouldn't try to provide extra warmth for them as it's simply not required.

LEAF LOSS

By now, you are probably aware that citrus trees have green leaves all year round, and they do drop *some* leaves from time to time, especially if the leaves are old. Citrus trees will naturally drop leaves during certain growing phases, such as blossoming and fruit formation.

Many people panic when they see leaf loss, but it's not entirely uncommon. It is, however, unusual if your tree is dropping a lot of leaves. Prolific leaf loss could be a sign of a more severe problem.

Possible causes of excessive leaf loss:

- Under-watering the tree
- Insufficient sunlight
- Soil nutrient deficiency
- Very dry soil with high salt content
- High heat
- Wind

HAND POLLINATION

It is most convenient that citrus flowers are self-pollinating. This is possible because the citrus flower is known as a "complete flower" – this means that both male and female reproductive parts are present within each citrus flower.

If you want your citrus tree's flowers to turn into fruit, they must be pollinated. There is no guarantee that every flower will self-pollinate successfully on the tree. The good news is that you increase the chances of fruit production by pollinating by hand. To do so, you need to know a little more about the biology of your citrus tree's flowers.

When the blooming season comes around, and the flowers open up on your citrus trees, take a look inside the flowers. Taking a look inside will reveal both male and female parts. Female flower parts are called the pistil and consist of the following:

- Stigma – this is the part of the pistil where pollen germinates. It is found at the very center of the flower
- Style – the style is the long tube-like section of the flower which is topped by the stigma

- Ovary – this is a bulb of the pistil where the ovules are produced in the flower

All of these are grouped together.

The male parts of the follower consist of the following:

- Stamen – this consists of a long slender stalk, the filament, and two-lobed anthers found at the very tip
- Filaments – the filament supports the pollen-producing anther
- Anthers – this is where the pollen is produced and is a bean-shaped (or lobed) structure on the top of the stamen

When a citrus tree self-pollinates, the anther releases pollen powder that falls onto the female stigma. Of course, if you are growing citrus trees indoors, they are protected from wind and insects/birds that may disturb the flower and cause the pollen to fall – this is why hand-pollination is the go-to for container gardeners.

One of the tell-tale signs that a flower has self-pollinated is when it closes and starts to wilt. If the flower doesn't wilt off but falls off the plant, pollination has not occurred.

Here's how to hand-pollinate your citrus tree's flowers for a more guaranteed yield:

- Identify the anther inside the flower
- Using a cotton swab or a small paintbrush, gently brush against the anther to dislodge some pollen
- Transfer the pollen powder from your cotton swab or bush onto the stigma

You will find that the stigma is quite sticky, and so traps the pollen powder.

Another way of hand-pollinating your citrus flowers is to shake the flower gently so that some pollen falls out onto your hand. Then press the pollen gently onto the stigma of the flower.

FLOWERING

Citrus trees flower at different times of the year. Most citrus trees flower once a year, but others blossom several times a year. Generally speaking, the smaller the fruit, the more often the tree may bloom during the year. For example, Navel Orange trees have quite big fruit and typically only bloom once a year in spring, whereas Lemons and Limes (some of them at least) can flower up to four times per year. When your citrus trees flower, it doesn't guarantee that they will produce fruit.

You may take a look at your citrus tree, see a myriad of flowers, and wonder how your tree will support so much fruit. When flowering does lead to fruit production, you can expect around 1% of the flowers to become fruit – there's no need to worry. Citrus trees are strategic planners in that they won't produce more fruit than they can handle. They don't want to be weighed down!

COMMON PESTS & DISEASES

While we go into more detail on the common pests that attack citrus trees in Chapter Six, here's a quick look at the common pests and diseases that may target your trees.

- Citrus Canker
- Aphids

- Leaf Miners
- Citrus Thrip
- Citrus White Fly
- Orangedog Caterpillars
- Snails
- Aphids
- Leaf Miners
- Mealy Bugs
- Citrus Scale
- Citrus Thrip
- Wasps
- Red Scale
- Melanose
- Greasy Spot
- Sooty Mold
- Root Rot
- Anthracnose
- Armillaria Root Rot
- Phytophthora Gummosis
- Blast
- Tristeza Disease

Of course, each citrus tree may vary. Pests that attack some citrus trees may not attack others. It's essential to check your citrus trees for pests and diseases regularly. Develop a habit of checking your citrus trees at least once a week so you are always aware of any possible problems developing (diseases and pests). Scrutinize the leaves, including the underside, and look for any webs or signs of insect life within the tree.

Please turn to Chapter Six for an in-depth description of each disease and pest and workable treatments for each.

PRUNING

The first thing I learned about pruning in citrus container gardening is that pruning isn't explicitly required. There is no reason that you *have to* prune your citrus trees, but pruning can prove helpful and beneficial to the tree. Below are a few reasons you may want to prune your citrus tree.

Size maintenance

Growing citrus trees in containers indoors means that you have limited space available. You may want to prune your citrus tree to maintain a manageable tree size for the available space. You can prune your tree to a smaller size but never remove more than 1/3 of the tree. By cutting too much off your citrus tree, you can stress it and also over-stimulate it.

Easier management and harvesting

Before you start pruning your citrus tree, you may notice that it has a lot of volume and growth that seems to go in all directions. The purpose of pruning will be to ensure that the fruits grow in a balanced format, making them easier to see throughout the growing process. With pruned branches, you will also be able to harvest your fruit with greater ease.

Allow sufficient light and air in

When your citrus tree has a lot of volume, it can be difficult for all the leaves to get sufficient air and light. By pruning branches, you can ensure that all the leaves get more air and light, allowing the tree to grow better and reduce stress.

Prevent overcrowding and cross branches

When a citrus tree is left to grow "wild", you may notice that it loses its ornamental appeal by growing branches that cross and crowd each other. If you want a citrus tree that looks aesthetically pleasing, use pruning to shape and form your tree.

Remove dead branches

Sometimes branches of a citrus tree die – that's just part of the process. You can prune these branches off to ensure that your tree always looks good.

Best Time to Prune

There's no point in pruning your citrus trees throughout the year. Instead, prune when there are unhealthy, unwanted, or inconveniently positioned branches. If you want to go by a pruning schedule, aim to prune soon after your winter harvest to early spring before new flower buds appear on the tree.

How to Prune Citrus Trees

You must use the correct equipment for pruning your citrus trees. Invest in some gloves, a good pair of pruning shears, and a hand-held saw (get a small one). Never use a regular pair of scissors for pruning.

Just in case of spreading disease and pests, make sure that you thoroughly disinfect your tools between uses and between trees.

Below are a few steps for pruning your citrus trees effectively:

- **Step one: strategize** - It's essential to prepare before you start pruning. Get up close to your citrus tree and examine it thoroughly. Note areas that are unhealthy and branches inconveniently located. Once you know what you need to do, gather your equipment to get started.
- **Step two: the pruning** - First off, remove any deadwood on the tree's branches. Remove thinner

branches, allowing the bigger/thicker branches to get even more robust. Only cut branches at 45-degree angles and be extra careful not to damage the central stalk.

- **Step three: remove skirting growth** - Skirting is the process of removing bottom growth to allow the canopy to thrive and fruit to prosper. Skirting also includes removing any under-developed fruit that's on the very bottom branches. Skirting serves another valuable purpose of ensuring that the leaves stay off the ground, avoiding contamination by fertilizers, and minimizing insects' opportunity to climb on board.

HUMIDITY

Citrus trees need humidity. Humidity for citrus trees is like a moisturizer for you.

Symptoms of low humidity:

- Dropping leaves
- Brittle leaf edges

Unfortunately, when winter comes around, your citrus trees aren't going to enjoy the dry indoor air. Enhancing the humidity in your citrus tree's environment will help it thrive and feel well-moisturized during the dry winter months. Here's how you can do that:

- Misting - Misting your citrus trees with a spray bottle filled with plain water will help create more humidity around the tree.
- Using a humidifier - If you don't have the time or

inclination to mist your trees every day, get a humidifier. This device should be placed close to your citrus trees when they are indoors for the winter.

- Using pebble trays - Placing a pebble tray beneath your citrus tree can increase the tree's humidity and ensure that it's never left wanting.

First of all, what is a pebble tray? It is simply a tray full of pebbles with water. While you can indeed find pebble trays for sale online, you can quite easily make your own.

All you need is a collection of small rocks, pebbles, or low-cost gravel and a shallow tray. I find that drainage saucers from old containers and pots work just as well. Fill the tray with your stones and add some water. Place the tray beneath your citrus tree container, and that's it! You only need to top up the tray with water when the water level drops.

HEAT/TEMPERATURES

It should come as no surprise that citrus trees like warm temperatures, but they can withstand a bit of cold if they have to. A citrus tree can handle temperatures as low as 39 degrees Fahrenheit (4 degrees Celsius). Of course, you don't want to push your trees to their limit because frost or freezing can lead to death. That said, citrus trees also handle high temperatures quite well. These trees flourish at 55 – 90 degrees Fahrenheit (12 – 32 degrees Celsius) but can withstand a few degrees higher.

It's imperative to note that your citrus trees should never have to experience extremes at either end of the spectrum. Even if the shock of scorching hot or freezing temperatures doesn't immediately kill the tree, it can suffer damage (or setback) that can be difficult to overcome.

Now that you know the basics, let's move onto Chapter Five, where we take a closer look at the care instructions for each type of citrus tree on our list.

5

CARE INSTRUCTIONS FOR
INDOOR CITRUS TREES

Keeping your potted citrus tree happy and healthy requires some planning and thought when it comes to positioning the plant and the amount of light and warmth it needs to flourish while indoors.

We have already touched on the importance of keeping your potted citrus away from radiators and underfloor heating. These conditions will dry out your pot too quickly, while a nasty draught will cause your citrus tree leaves to turn yellow or brown and possibly drop off.

If your potted citrus tree is healthy and happy, its leaves will be shiny and glossy. The leaves can require an occasional clean.

You can do this using some dishwashing liquid in warm water - gently clean the leaves with a sponge.

While your tree is indoors during the winter months, it is acceptable for the temperature to drop to around 41 – 50 degrees Fahrenheit (5 – 10 degrees Celsius).

While these are the basic steps to keep your citrus tree happy, each species has its own specific needs. Specific care instructions for each of the citrus trees we're focusing on are detailed below.

KUMQUATS

Particular details of Kumquat tree care are below.

Sunlight

With your Kumquat tree planted in suitable soil and container, it will flourish in bright natural light or even direct sunlight. The sunlight will discourage leaf molds and fungus from infecting your citrus tree, encouraging vibrant growth and vigor. Give your Kumquat a lot of sunlight if you want it to thrive, leading to sumptuous fruit development.

Place your tree close to an insulated window but not with the leaves touching the glass. Kumquats love a balmy 68 degrees Fahrenheit (20 degrees Celsius), and although they are happy with lower temperatures at night, they will thrive in warm south-facing rooms.

Humidity

The leaves require moisture and will benefit from light daily misting with a spray bottle which will boost the humidity but will not risk over-watering the tree. If keeping the humidity level constant at about 50% – 60% proves difficult for you, it is advisable to use a humidifier. If it is wintertime and the central heating is on, then misting the leaves will probably be enough to keep your Kumquat tree happy.

Another way to provide your Kumquat tree with humidity is with a pebble tray. Place a shallow tray filled with pebbles and water beneath your pot/container and as the water level lowers, simply top it up. This will provide your tree with sufficient humidity.

Air circulation

Kumquat trees need good air circulation, so it is good to raise the pot off the ground. Using a container on wheels is perfect, especially when you want to move your tree to a different position, but if this is not possible, perhaps stand the container on some blocks or feet. Using this method will also stop the roots from standing in water, which is not ideal for citrus trees.

Water

Kumquat trees are no exception to the rule that citrus trees do not like "wet feet", so the drainage must be perfect. How often you need to water your tree depends on a few factors, like location to light and darkness, the room temperature, and your tree's size in relation to its container. Never let the soil dry out; water regularly, but as a rule, keeping the soil slightly moist will keep your Kumquat tree thriving.

If you have under-watered, the tree will begin to stress, and this will cause the leaves to curl and lose their glossy color. If the soil is dry when you touch it, it is a sign it needs to be watered. That deals with under-watering, but what do you look for if you have been overwatering the tree? Over-watering is, unfortunately, the cause of root rot which leads to the death of the tree.

Fertilizer

Everyone needs food and sustenance, and so does your Kumquat tree. Fertilizing with a high-quality citrus fertilizer will encourage your tree to grow and flower. The ideal fertilizing time is at the beginning of the growing season. Kumquat trees love seaweed extract, and it is a good idea to use a watered-down liquid fertilizer, specially made for citrus trees once a month.

Getting it outside

When the weather gets warmer, which is from spring to summer, the height of the growing season, you will want to give your Kumquat tree some more direct sunlight. This will mean moving it outside to a sheltered sunny area. After being inside for a few months, this process needs to be done in stages.

The first step is to put your tree outside in the house's shade with some shelter or under a larger tree. When the kumquat tree has acclimatized to the sunny weather, then ensure it gets plenty of direct sunlight.

When the summer starts to fade to fall, it is time to bring your tree back indoors. You will need to start by placing it in the shade of the house or tree again for a few days, so it becomes accustomed to low light again, and then bring it back indoors.

LEMONS

Particular care instructions for Lemon trees are below.

Sunlight

Like all citrus trees, indoor Lemon trees need a lot of sunlight or direct light, ideally positioned in the sunniest window in the house. If your Lemon tree doesn't get enough light, it will not flower and produce fruit. Lemon trees need between 8 and 12 hours of sunlight a day. If you can't provide this for your Lemon tree naturally, it might be an option to assist your Lemon tree with a grow light.

Keep your Lemon tree cozy and warm when indoors, but avoid placing it near any radiators, ovens, or fireplaces. Constant temperature control is best to keep it thriving as Lemon trees do not like a quick change in temperatures.

Lemon trees thrive indoors at a temperature of 70 – 100 degrees Fahrenheit (21 – 38 degrees Celsius), do not allow it to get too warm as this will stop your Lemon tree from growing. Also, be careful that it doesn't get too cold as it will cause your Lemon tree to go into dormancy.

Humidity

For your Lemon tree to flourish, you will need to have the humidity at 50%, which can be a mission for any home to maintain, but you can hack this by using the following methods:

- Humidifier
- Pebble tray
- Misting the leaves
- Air circulation

Natural air movement is essential for the happiness of your Lemon tree. If it is not possible to open a window to promote air circulation, then perhaps use a small fan or ceiling fan in the room to encourage good air movement. Good air circulation will also help reduce pest infestations.

Although creating good airflow is essential, make sure your Lemon tree does not get cold or chilly, so ensure the fan or open window does not cast air not directly on your tree.

Water

It is advisable to have a layer of mulch on the top of the container soil, pebbles, or decorative mulch to reduce evaporation and aid in water retention. Regular watering is the idea but do not over-water as the Lemon tree's roots do not like to sit in water - the roots need air, and if overloaded with water, it will lead to root rot.

Drainage is essential, so when watering, ensure the water runs freely out the drainage holes and then stop watering. The rule of thumb, in this case, is to keep the soil damp but not wet to the touch — only water when the soil's top layer is drying out. You might water twice a week in the summer months while in winter months, perhaps only once every two weeks.

Fertilizer

To keep it simple for an indoor potted Lemon tree, use liquid fertilizer, giving the Lemon tree the nutrients it needs to grow and thrive indoors. From spring to summer, feed your tree every three weeks. From fall to winter, feed your tree every 1.5 weeks.

A liquid fertilizer high in nitrogen is recommended for citrus trees and works best but be careful not to over-fertilize as this will cause a chemical burn to the tree. If you see yellow spots, called chlorophyll, on your Lemon tree, it is an indicator of stress, which means your tree needs more nutrients.

Getting it outside

Being outside in the fresh air and direct sunlight is the best life you can give your Lemon tree. This will assist with the humidity and air circulation for the growth and health of the tree. When deciding to relocate your Lemon tree outside, make sure it's a slow and steady process, taking time to acclimatize the tree to outdoors and the temperature change.

Begin when the last frost has gone and only for a few hours on a sunny day. Keep your tree sheltered from the wind and excessive sun when the weather warms up, then leave the Lemon tree outside under the shelter of a larger tree or the house's protection.

When fully acclimatized, let your Lemon tree enjoy a sheltered sunny place with good airflow. As the weather turns back to fall, reverse the process and start bringing your Lemon tree back indoors to protect from the frost and winter weather.

LIMES

Particular care instructions for Lime trees are below.

Sunlight

Lime trees are tropical trees that enjoy warmth and lots of sunshine. Place your indoor tree in a bright sunny, south-facing window. Do not panic if you cannot guarantee your Lime tree 6 – 8 hours of light. To sort this problem, try using a grow light. The consequence of having insufficient light will be that your tree will not flower or bear fruit.

If you go this route, choose a tall LED light that will supply enough light and a little warmth replicating sunshine. Leave the light on for at least 8 hours which will be long enough to encourage flowering and the fruit to set without the tree becoming stressed.

Humidity

Like all citrus trees, Lime trees are no different. They require a constant humidity level. Humidity is optimal, and you can achieve this by misting the tree every few days to lift the humidity level. As is the case with Kumquat and Lemon trees, the following methods can be used to create sufficient humidity:

- Humidifier
- Pebble tray
- Misting the leaves

If using a humidifier, place it close to your Lime tree for the best results.

Air circulation

Place your Lime tree in a well-ventilated room away from fire-places, radiators, and underfloor heating. When the weather permits, open the windows or door to allow good air circulation in the room. If the weather does not allow opening the windows or door, then try placing a fan in the room but not blowing directly on the tree.

Pruning is another way of encouraging airflow in the tree's crown and allows more light onto the middle branches, helping the fruit to ripen.

You can prune your indoor Lime tree any time of the year except when flowering or bearing fruit.

Water

Knowing the exact amount of water needed for an indoor Lime tree is to follow the rule of keeping the tree moist but never soggy. Lime trees do not like standing in water so ensure your drainage holes are working well. Occasionally your Lime tree might enjoy a thorough soaking instead of regular shallow watering.

To achieve this, water the tree until the water runs out the drainage holes, allowing all excess water to drain away. An easy health check on your Lime tree's watering needs is to take note of the leaves. If they are yellowing and curling, it means you are over-watering, leading to root rot (caused by a bacterial infection). If you suspect root rot, it is essential to re-pot your Lime tree as soon as possible to save it.

If the leaves are wilting and drooping, then you have under-watered your tree. The solution to this would be to give your Lime tree a deep watering, and then the foliage should return to normal.

Fertilizer

Not only does your Lime tree enjoy light and watering, but it also appreciates a good fertilizer. If possible, use a fertilizer specially formulated for indoor citrus trees at least once a month. Ensure it is high in zinc, iron, and manganese.

Granular slow-release fertilizer is best, but liquid versions work too. Start applying fertilizer in late winter or early spring and continue until growth starts to slow in late summer or early fall.

Getting it outside

When the weather warms up, it will be perfect for getting your Lime tree outside but be careful not to shock your tree with a dramatic temperature change. The best time to start moving your Lime tree outside is when there is no frost or cold temperatures in the spring.

Acclimatize your Lime tree by slowly introducing it to the outdoors. Place it in a sheltered position away from the wind and extreme sun, and choose dappled sun to begin with, then eventually, when the Lime tree has acclimatized, it will cope with full sun.

If the temperatures still fall below 24 degrees Fahrenheit (-4 degrees Celsius) at night or day for any length of time, it is best to bring your Lime tree indoors or cover it to protect it.

ORANGES

Particular care instructions for Orange trees are below.

Sunlight

Light is vital for your Orange tree. Placing it at a south-facing window to receive as much natural sunlight as possible will help your tree thrive. Your Orange tree needs at least 5 – 6 hours of good daylight. If placed at a window, check if the glass is hot to the touch; this means there is sufficient sunlight for your Orange tree to thrive.

If not, then do not despair, as this can be solved using a grow light to extend the hours of light your Orange tree needs. Resist the urge to keep your Orange tree warm and cozy by placing it near a radiator as this will only dry your Orange tree out. Instead, keep it in a bright sunny room out of the way of draughts or rapid temperature changes.

Humidity

Humidity is fundamental in keeping your Orange tree healthy, try and keep this at 50% – 70% to encourage blossoming. This humidity level is similar to the natural tropical environment for an Orange tree.

Although Orange trees like the warmth, it is best if it is not a dry heat, so the humidity level keeps the tree cool while enjoying the heat. The most suitable rooms for this are the kitchen or bathroom. It will be the ideal warmth and humidity if you can put your Orange tree in one of these rooms.

To assist with humidity, you can use the following methods:

- Humidifier
- Pebble tray
- Misting the leaves
- Air circulation

Sufficient air circulation is crucial for keeping your Orange tree happy. At the same time, you can ensure you maintain good circulation around your Orange tree; it will reciprocate by improving the air quality of your home.

Pruning or thinning out the center of your Orange tree will also promote good air circulation for the tree.

Water

One top tip to share is that you should never let an indoor Orange tree dry out. The consequence of this is that the roots will die. Ensure the pot you have planted your tree in is big enough and has plenty of drainage holes. Like other citrus trees, Orange trees do not grow if their roots are standing in water.

When you water your Orange tree, try and have the water at room temperature. If the water is hot or too cold, it will "shock" the tree, resulting in death or poor growth. A tree in shock might never recover or thrive.

You will need to water your Orange tree more regularly in summer than in winter. Your tree will start to slow down growth in winter and will not need as much water.

Orange trees love natural rainwater, so if you can, perhaps place a container outside when it's raining to give your Orange tree a treat.

Fertilizer

Orange trees are very hungry and need feeding regularly. You should feed your Orange tree with a high potassium feed and liquid seaweed fertilizer once a week during the summer. During the winter months, feed your Orange tree every fortnight.

Your Orange tree will then reward you with an abundance of blossoms and fruit. An Orange tree will need feeding all through the year as it does not go dormant. Orange trees always need additional micronutrients, more than ordinary citrus fertilizers contain, so ensure you supplement manganese, zinc, and iron in your fertilizer regime.

Getting it outside

In the warmer months, spoil your Orange tree to some time outside – move it to the patio or in a sheltered warm spot in the garden. Your tree will benefit from the sunlight and natural air circulation at these times, and it will also control any disease or pests on your tree, helping to keep it healthy and strong.

During summer, the optimal outdoor temperatures are between 46 – 86 degrees Fahrenheit (8 – 30 degrees Celsius). When the cooler weather starts to creep back, it is time to bring your Orange tree back inside.

A conservatory or a greenhouse, if you have one, is ideal for putting your Orange tree in when temperatures fall below 50 degrees Fahrenheit (10 degrees Celsius) for a while (longer than 10 hours will be detrimental to the Orange tree).

MANDARINS

Particular care instructions for Mandarin trees are below.

Sunlight

Sunlight or natural light is vital when growing your Mandarin tree indoors. It will greatly benefit your tree's growth and fruiting if you place the tree next to the sunniest window, in the brightest room of the house. If you cannot provide your Mandarin tree with this, then invest in some grow lights. These will work well but need to be on for 8 – 10 hours per day to be of any benefit.

Although your Mandarin tree needs sunlight, please do not put it next to a radiator or central heating as this will only dry your tree out too quickly.

Humidity

A little-known fact about Mandarin trees is that they thrive in humidity. They will tolerate drier soil but need as much humidity as possible, especially in winter when the central heating is on, and the air is dry. It is recommended you spritz your Mandarin tree leaves every so often to keep the moisture up. You can also use the following methods to keep humidity levels up:

- Humidifier
- Pebble tray
- Air circulation

Air circulation is important for the health of your Mandarin tree, especially if it is indoors. Adequate circulation will ensure no pests or fungal infestations will attack your tree. If possible, open a window if the weather allows, or move your tree outside if the weather is mild for it to benefit from natural air circulation. If this is not possible, consider putting a fan in the room to circulate the air or have a ceiling fan operating on low for a few hours to assist with circulation.

Water

Mandarin trees are more drought tolerant than you think, be careful not to over-water and rather under-water the tree. Mandarin trees, like all citrus, hate wet roots, so let your tree dry out between watering.

The pot must have suitable drainage holes with an appropriate draining potting mix. When it has dried out, water your Mandarin tree by drenching the soil so it pours out the drainage holes. Watering requirements will increase in summer to once or twice a week and decrease in winter to once a fortnight.

Fertilizer

Like all citrus trees, Mandarins are no exception to the rule; they need feeding to reap blossoms and fruit rewards. Use a slightly nitrogen-rich citrus fertilizer or a balanced NPK fertilizer, where possible. Potted Mandarins need more food than trees in the ground. Mandarins enjoy a slow-release fertilizer. When your Mandarin tree is indoors, fertilize once a month and twice a month when the tree is outdoors.

Getting it outside

Mandarin trees in pots can be grown successfully outdoors for most of the year, only requiring to be moved indoors when the temperatures start to fall in the fall.

During the summer months, you can move your Mandarin tree outdoors onto the patio or decking and position your tree so it gets the full morning sun until the early afternoon. From around midday, the hottest part of the day, you will need to move your tree into the shade to avoid leaf burn and heat stress.

In fall, when the evening temperatures start to fall, it is time to move your Mandarin tree back indoors.

6

COMMON CITRUS TREE
PROBLEMS & SOLUTIONS

I n my time as an avid gardener, I have come to learn that it's one thing to know what diseases and insects negatively impact citrus trees in general. It's quite something else to recognize a problem and know how to treat it. When you know what you're looking for and can immediately jump into action, you can save the life of your citrus tree without wasting any time.

By familiarizing yourself with the various pests and diseases that plague citrus trees, you can cut out a lot of the guesswork regarding treatment. You can also eliminate confusion. Nothing is worse than watching your citrus tree dying and not knowing what you can do to help it.

The following section focuses on taking a closer look at each type of disease and pest plaguing citrus trees today. Each section provides information on what issues to look out for, warning signs to be aware of, and solutions to try.

Please make use of the QR codes below by using the camera function on your phone - you will be directed to a website / Google images for your benefit.

PESTS THAT TARGET CITRUS TREES

Mealybugs

Affects:

- **Kumquat Trees**
- **Orange Trees**

Mealybugs are flat and soft-bodied with sharp sucking mouths. They feed on the sap of the citrus tree. Their feeding process reduces the tree's ability to transport nutrients and moisture to all parts, which, as you can imagine, is quite detrimental to its overall health and productivity. They also excrete a sweet substance (honeydew) that attracts ants. If you notice ants feeding on a sticky substance on your trees, look out for Mealy-bugs. If left untreated, mold can develop from the honeydew and spread over the leaves, deterring photosynthesis.

What to look for:

- Yellowing leaves
- Leaf drop
- Distorted growth
- Sooty Black Mold

Solution:

You can control these pests on citrus trees organically or chemically. If you choose to use an organic treatment, you can use a hose (with a hard spray) on the tree's leaves early each morning. This creates an unpleasant environment for pests to live in by knocking them off.

Most insects won't find their way back to the tree, but if they do, consistent rinsing of the tree will eventually become too much for them. You can also introduce natural predators such as lady beetles, lacewings, and syrphid flies. For a chemical solution, you can apply an insecticide to the tree that contains chlorpyrifos or make a solution of veg-based oil and dishwashing liquid to spray onto the tree.

Leaf Miners

Affects:

- **Mandarin Trees**
- **Kumquats Trees**
- **Lemon Trees**
- **Lime Trees**
- **Orange Trees**

Leaf Miners are opportunistic moths that lay their eggs underneath the leaf. When the larvae hatch, they dig down into the leaf, making "mining" tunnels. Leaf Miners can be detrimental to young citrus trees (younger than three years). It's worth noting that the most older, more established trees, Leaf Miners are merely a nuisance.

What to look for:

- White or silvery pattern twisting and turning all over the leaf's surface
- Curling leaves
- Leaf drop

Solution:

You can use either an organic or chemical solution for this particular problem. The Leaf Miner has several natural predators, including parasitic wasps, so capitalize on this. You should also prune off affected leaves and dispose of them far from your citrus trees.

If you prefer to use a chemical treatment, a horticultural oil sprayed every ten days should be fine. One thing to note is not to use oil sprays when the temperatures are over 26 degrees Celsius (80 degrees Fahrenheit), as this can cause damage to the plant. You can also look for insecticides that contain Spinosad.

Citrus Scale

Affects:

- **Mandarin Trees**
- **Kumquat Trees**
- **Lemon Trees**
- **Lime Trees**
- **Orange Trees**

Citrus Scales are tiny sap-sucking insects that leave a sticky honeydew residue on the tree's leaves. If left untreated, the honeydew attracts ants which can result in the demise of the tree. Two main types of Citrus Scale may attack your citrus tree. These are the Armored Citrus Scale and Soft Citrus Scale. The Armored Citrus Scale inserts its mouth into the leaf and fruit of the citrus tree and simply never moves. Soft Scale Citrus Scale are similar but can move about freely.

What to look for:

- Disfigured fruit
- Waxy buildup on leaves and fruit
- Leaf drop
- Branch dieback

Solution:

First, remove any affected branches and leaves. To treat Citrus Scale organically, you can use natural predators such as the lacewing or lady beetles. Another organic route is to use environmentally friendly pesticides that include insecticidal soap or d-Limonene. These need to be applied frequently to be effective. If you plan to use chemicals, you can use a neem-based oil dabbed or sprayed onto the leaves for light infestations. You can also look for insecticide sprays that contain Azadirachtin.

Aphids

Affects:

- **Kumquat Trees**
- **Lemon Trees**
- **Lime Trees**
- **Mandarin Trees**
- **Orange Trees**

Aphids are tiny insects that are almost invisible at a glance. On closer inspection, you may see them. They are soft-bodied insects that can appear green, white, yellow, grey, brown, black, or pink. Aphids have a sharp sucking mouth which they use to drain the leaves of sap. Aphids tend to multiply fast and will destroy your citrus tree if left untreated.

What to look for:

- Leaf and flower drop
- Yellowing and curling leaves
- Sticky substance on leaves
- Sooty Black Mold on leaves

Solution:

Organic ways of dealing with Aphids include blasting the tree with cool water every day to make it an unsuitable environment for them. You can also dust the tree with flour or use an insecticide that includes DE (Diatomaceous Earth). Alternative treatments involve spraying the tree down with a weak dishwashing liquid and water solution or spraying neem oil or other horticultural oil on the tree leaves.

Thrips

Affects:

- **Lemon Trees**
- **Mandarin Trees**

Thrips can target citrus trees all year round. Thrips are yellow or light green and are pretty small, measuring less than 5mm each. They feed on young leaves and fruit and, interestingly enough, cannot survive on mature foliage alone. The feeding activity of Thrips scars the fruit skin as they feed on the fruit bud and punctures the cells in the rind to get to the sap inside.

The eggs are typically laid in the soft leaf tissue or young fruit, so these are areas to focus on when spraying the tree.

What to look for:

- Damage to the calyx in the form of a silvery-white blemish
- Mature fruit has brown damage around the calyx
- Severe fruit rind scarring
- Stunted tree growth

Solution:

Never use broad-spectrum insecticides to treat thrips as they tend to kill natural predators of thrips. Many people use a broad-spectrum insecticide and notice the Thrip population increases shortly after. For an organic treatment, choose an insecticide with Spinosad listed in the contents and spray your trees in early spring. For chemical treatment, look for insecticides with Organophosphates and Pyrethroids in the contents.

Snails

Affects:

- **Kumquat Trees**
- **Lemon Trees**
- **Lime Trees**
- **Mandarin Trees**
- **Orange Trees**

Snails are known to cause considerable damage to citrus trees by feeding on the fruit and leaves. They also feed on the bark of young citrus trees. Snails are largely inactive during the summer. Rainfall typically triggers snail activity (watering can have the same effect if snails are sheltering in tree canopies). The fall is when snails usually begin moving around, mating, feeding, and laying eggs. They do a lot of laying in winter, but moist soil deters this. Snails are more active when the day is at its coolest, so do monitoring in the early morning and at night to determine how big your snail problem is.

What to look for:

- Circular chewed parts on the rind
- Damaged leaves along the margins

Solution:

There are several things you can do to deter snails from getting comfortable on your citrus trees. A popular method is to prune tree skirts so that snails don't have easy access. At the same time, wrap your tree's trunk in copper foil or copper sulfate. This prevents the snail from climbing up into the tree. Snail bait that contains Methiocarb, Iron EDTA, and Metaldehyde is popular, but it is important to note that these are poisonous to both pets and humans (not a good idea if you have children or pets).

. . .

Mites

Affects:

- **Kumquat Trees**
- **Lemon Trees**
- **Lime Trees**
- **Mandarin Trees**
- **Orange Trees**

Citrus mites come in two primary forms; red mites and rust mites. Rust mites typically attack the leaves, whereas red mites attack the fruit. Citrus mites are very small (sometimes not even 1mm in size) and come in various colors, including red, rusty-red, yellow, and brown. The mites feed on the leaves of fruit trees as well as green twigs. In most instances, you will see webbing on the plant as a telltale sign, but the Citrus Red Mite sometimes produces very little or no webbing at all.

What to look for:

- Webbing (almost like a spider web)
- Leaves become spotted with yellow necrotic areas
- Fruit rind has black or dark brown patches
- Distorted and undersized fruit
- Yellowing of the leaves

Solutions:

If your citrus tree already has a Citrus Mite infestation, it is essential to prune the affected areas and destroy the debris. Spray a horticultural spray or insecticidal soap on the tree. You can also make a mix of water, dishwashing detergent, and veg-based oil to spray on the tree. Treating the tree before it blooms is usually adequate, but if you spray after the tree is infested or the galls have developed, the treatment will be of no use.

DISEASES THAT PLAGUE CITRUS TREES

Please scan the QR codes below to view images of each disease mentioned.

Alternaria Leaf Spots

Affects:

- **Kumquat Trees**
- **Orange Trees**
- **Lemon Trees**

Alternaria leaf spots are plaque-like spots that appear on the leaves of the citrus tree. The disease is actually a fungus infection that can be very difficult to get rid of once it's taken hold of the plant.

What to look for:

- Small dark spots (less than 1cm diameter) spreading across leaves
- Spots turning black with a yellow halo
- Leaf wilt
- Leaf drop
- Weakened plant
- Unsightly lesions

While most plant fungi cannot be harmful to humans, some do produce toxins, so it's best not to eat fruit with Alternaria spots on them.

Solution:

Treating Alternaria Leaf Spot requires both a preventative and curing approach. To prevent infection, avoid watering your tree from overhead to limit how wet the leaves get. Also, space your trees out to ensure good air circulation. Clear up all fallen debris and leaves. Captan and copper-based fungicides are the best possible response to Alternaria Leaf Spot.

Anthracnose

Affects:

- **Kumquat Trees**
- **Lemon Trees**
- **Orange Trees**
- **Mandarin Trees**

Anthracnose is a fungus that is quickly passed on from one plant (or garden tool) to another. It is spread by watering and thrives in moist or warm conditions. You may find that you only have this problem in the cooler months as Anthracnose can become dormant when the weather is warm.

What to look for:

- Branch dieback
- Premature leaf dropping
- Dark marks on the fruit
- Dark fungal spots on the leaves

Solution:

If your citrus tree has Anthracnose, remove any parts of the plant affected and discard them. Spray your citrus tree with a copper-based fungicide, but don't do this too regularly, as too much copper in the soil can become toxic to earthworms.

European Brown Rot

Affects:

- **Lemon Trees**
- **Mandarin Trees**
- **Lime Trees**

European Brown Rot is an unforgiving disease that must be dealt with as soon as fruits and leaves have fallen off and you're preparing for the following seasons. The condition is caused by a fungus and causes a severely detrimental impact on fruit harvests. The disease targets the fruit, making them rot off before they mature. You will find that European Brown Rot usually shows up in spring, and like most fungal diseases, moisture is what triggers it.

What to look for:

- Brown blemishes on the fruit
- Fruit that's soft and mushy
- Wrinkled fruit that's rotting

- Grayish fruit that doesn't drop from the tree

Solution:

Treating European Brown Rot must include a preventative approach, so start treating against the disease in the fall, when the fruit and leaves typically fall from the tree. Then approach your treatment strategy in stages. Be very careful when dealing with fruit with this disease as wind propagates the seeds, which can overwinter, ready for the next season!

Spray the tree with a Boudeaux mix every two to three weeks in fall and winter. In the spring, use a fruit tree disease treatment spray that contains Fenbuconazole. Spray with this when the tree is blooming so that Brown Rot doesn't have a chance. If your tree falls prey to the disease, burn all affected leaves and fruit after the season and spray your tree.

Greasy Spot

Affects:

- **Kumquats**
- **Lemon Trees**
- **Orange Trees**
- **Lime Trees**

- **Mandarin Trees**

Greasy Spot is a fungal disease affecting the leaves of citrus trees. The fungus may appear harmless enough, but if you leave it untreated, the tree will lose all of its leaves and eventually die off. The fungus typically survives in crop debris (fallen leaves) on the soil surface, and in the spring when the weather gets a bit warmer, all it takes is a few splashes of water to activate them. The wind propagates the spores. When landing on the underside of a leaf, the spores germinate, and fungi penetrate the leaves' tissues through their pores. Infection usually happens in late spring to early summer, and you may not even notice the first signs until the start of winter.

What to look for:

- Raised yellow-brown (or orange) blisters on the underside of the leaves
- Gradually blisters show on the top of the leaf
- Black spots on leaves and fruit that appear greasy
- Leaf drop
- Diminished fruit production

Solution:

The good news is that treating Greasy Spot is fairly simple. You can spray the tree thoroughly with a copper-based fungicide. You may notice that the tree drops a few leaves after spraying – don't stress about this.

Citrus Canker

Affects:

- **Lemon Trees**
- **Lime Trees**
- **Orange Trees**
- **Mandarin Trees**

Citrus Canker is a disease that has been devastating to the citrus market numerous times. It's particularly prevalent in areas where there's a lot of rainfall and the temperatures are warm. In mild cases, the disease may only affect the fruit rind and the leaves, but if the condition is severe, it can cause the total demise of the citrus tree. Kumquats are particularly resistant to Citrus Canker.

What to look for:

- Premature leaf drop
- Fruit drop
- Branch and dieback
- Blemished fruit
- Blister-like lesion son the leaves and fruit (tan or black with a yellow halo)

Solution:

It's interesting to note that there is no actual cure for Citrus Canker. The best way of protecting your trees from the disease is to take preventative measures. Regularly spraying your citrus trees with copper-based fungicides is the only way. You can also introduce windbreaks to your garden to ensure that spores don't move from tree to tree. If your tree has already contracted Citrus Canker, prune the affected areas off the tree and burn the debris.

Sooty Mold Fungus

Affects:

- **Kumquat Trees**
- **Lemon Trees**
- **Orange Trees**
- **Lime Trees**
- **Mandarin Trees**

Sooty Mold Fungus is a powdery black fungus that grows on the fruit, leaves, and branches of citrus trees. If you see Sooty Mold Fungus on your citrus trees, it's a sign that your tree has fallen prey to harmful insects (sap-sucking insects in particular), so pay close attention to your tree. The good news is that the mold isn't hazardous but can be unsightly.

What to look for:

- Powdery black mold on the leaves

Solution:

When trying to treat your citrus ree for Sooty Mold Fungus, first try to figure out what insect has invaded your tree. Once you have a better idea of that information, you need to treat your tree for that particular insect. Once the insect infestation is under control, the Sooty Mold Fungus should gradually wear off. If you want to speed up the process, you can blast the tree with water or with a mix of dishwashing detergent and water to wash the appearance off the leaves.

Black Root Rot

Affects:

- **Kumquats**
- **Lemon Trees**
- **Orange Trees**
- **Lime Trees**

- **Mandarin Trees**

Black Root Rot is a disease that you shouldn't overlook as it's pretty severe to the health of your citrus tree. This is a soil-borne fungus disease that is prolific in damp soil. Left untreated, it will cause the slow decline and eventual death of your citrus tree. Young trees and seedlings take the most significant knock from Black Root Rot, and you will find that the disease does the most damage during the spring.

What to look for:

- Stunted new leaf growth
- Branch dieback
- Yellowing leaves between veins
- Leaf drop
- Black lesions on the roots

Solution:

Prevention is better than cure when it comes to treating Black Root Rot. If the soil of your citrus tree is very wet, let it dry out before watering it again. You can drench your soil with water containing Triflumizole, Methyl, and Fludioxonil. If your citrus tree contracts Black Root Rot while still potted, remove it from the pot, trim off the black root sections, and then re-pot the tree in fresh, sterile soil. Withhold watering until the soil dries out. Providing your tree with enough sunlight will also help to prevent Black Root Rot from setting in. Well-draining soil is also essential.

Blast

Affects:

- **Kumquat Trees**
- **Lemon Trees**
- **Orange Trees**
- **Mandarins**

Citrus Blast is a disease that's also called "Black Pit" or "Bacterial Blast." It's a bacterial infection that usually presents after high wind and rainfall. The bacteria that causes this disease is opportunistic in that it enters the plant through punctures, blemishes, and insect feeding sites on the plant.

What to look for:

- Reddish-brown scabs in the diseased areas
- Small black spots on the fruit
- Branch dieback
- Leaf drop

Solutions:

Treating Citrus Blast is simple. All you need to do is spray your trees with a copper-based spray. As some strains have become resistant to treatments, you can boost effectiveness by adding

Ferric Chloride or Mancozeb to Cupric Hydroxic and applying it to the tree. You can also incorporate windbreaks in your garden to protect the citrus tree from strong winds.

Tristeza Disease

Affects:

- **Orange Trees**
- **Mandarin Trees**
- **Lime Trees**
- **Lemon Trees**

Tristeza Disease is a decline syndrome that results from CTV (Citrus Tristeza Virus) on citrus trees that are propagated on the rootstocks of oranges and lemons. Aphids commonly spread the disease.

What to look for:

- Light green leaves
- Poor growth
- Pitted stems
- Leaf cupping
- Leaf drop

- Undersized fruit
- Feeder roots dying off

Solutions:

One of the best ways to avoid this problem is to buy trees that haven't been grafted and avoid grafting, especially on Orange and Lemon rootstocks. Spray the tree in neem oil to reduce the risk of Aphids being present and spreading the disease.

Phytophthora Gummosis

Affects:

- **Kumquats**
- **Lemon Trees**
- **Orange Trees**
- **Lime Trees**
- **Mandarin Trees**

This disease is caused by fungi and affects all types of citrus trees. The disease, which is a soil-borne infection, occurs from the ground level up and affects the entire tree, the root system included. Most citrus trees with the disease die within a year, but there are instances where the disease slowly takes the tree over several years. When the condition is severe, it will affect the fruit as well.

What to look for:

- Sap oozing from cracks in the tree stem/bark
- Bark dries out and falls off
- Yellowing leaves
- Leaf drop
- Dying feeder roots

Solutions:

Bark trimming is one of the best ways to eliminate this disease from citrus trees. Trimming requires you to remove the diseased bark from the tree. Strip the bark away until you only see healthy bark left behind. Once this is done, allow the wound to dry and keep checking to see if the infection has come back. If it does, trim it out again. Using fungicides regularly can also prevent the problem. It's also a good preventative measure to have well-draining soil.

Now that you're familiar with the common diseases and pests plaguing citrus trees and what you can do about it, let's move onto our next section, which deals with transplanting your citrus tree into the garden.

7

TRANSPLANTING CITRUS TREES TO THE GARDEN

There comes a stage in most citrus container gardeners' lives when they wish to see their citrus tree flourish and thrive in the "wild", and so the idea of transplanting the tree into the garden comes to mind. If your citrus tree seems to be outgrowing its container and you can't find a solution (sometimes there aren't pots large enough), transplanting your citrus tree is the next logical step. The good news is your tree will be fine outside, thanks to your care and maintenance over all this time.

By now, you might believe that your citrus tree is deceptively hardy, but it's important to note that transplanting a citrus tree is a delicate task. You have to do it just right if you want your tree to do well in its new environment. Keep the following in mind when transplanting your citrus tree.

TIMING

One of the first things I want to tell you is that timing is everything when transplanting a citrus tree. You may look at your tree and think it's time to get it relocated, but if the weather isn't great, your citrus tree is going to experience shock at the sudden change. The ideal time to transplant your trees is in the spring. This is just before the summer heat starts to beat down, but also after the coldest parts of winter have passed.

To avoid the roots drying out and suffering a negative impact, aim to transplant your trees in the early morning. You should also avoid transplanting your citrus trees into the garden within their first year of life.

DEPTH OF THE HOLE

The hole you dig for your citrus tree needs to be prepared well. To say that a citrus tree is fussy would be an understatement. Before you take your tree out of the pot, spend some time working on the hole. First, you need to dig a hole of around 18 –25in (45 – 60cm) deep.

The citrus tree gets most of its food and water from feeder roots – these roots will be within the first 18in of soil, so keep this in mind. It's also crucial that you test the hole for drainage – remember that citrus trees like good drainage, so water must drain well from the hole reasonably quickly.

Fill the hole with water once it's dug and monitor how quickly the water drains away. If the soil doesn't drain well, your citrus tree will not be happy at all. You may have to select a different location. If you are planting more than one citrus tree, keep in mind that the trees must be situated at least 59in apart (1.5m).

POST-TRANSPLANT CARE

When your citrus tree is in its new space, it's probably going to go into shock. That's relatively normal, but if it doesn't pep up in a few days, that's not a good sign. To ensure that your citrus tree quickly becomes happy again, you need to provide it with the proper care. Below are a few tips for caring for your newly transplanted citrus tree.

Watering

A newly planted citrus tree needs watering regularly, especially if there isn't sufficient rainfall. Also, keep in mind that when you water your tree in a pot, it has access to more water than when you're watering it outside in the garden (this is due to the way the water will flow and drain naturally – without a pot to control it). Avoid overwatering by allowing the soil to almost dry out between watering, and make sure that you thoroughly drench the soil when next watering your tree.

Feeding the soil

You shouldn't add any fertilizer to the soil when you transplant your citrus tree. Only start adding fertilizer to the soil once the tree has settled (you can wait around a month). Fertilize your transplanted citrus tree every 3 – 4 months.

When transplanting your tree, you can use compost to provide added nutrition to the soil.

Disease and pest prevention

Now that your citrus tree is outside, it is exposed to more infections and pests than ever before. You don't have to buy expensive sprays and poisons to keep your trees problem-free. You can make your own sprays using household ingredients. Here are a few easy-to-make options:

Oil and Spice Spray

Mix one cup of veg-based oil in 4 liters of water. Add a tablespoon of cinnamon oil and mix well. For the mixture to be even more effective, add two tablespoons of chili powder in 2 cups of water, strain it, and add the liquid to the mix. Lastly, add three tablespoons of dishwashing detergent to the mixture. Using a spray bottle, apply this to the tree - spray the tree thoroughly every second week.

Oil and Soap Spray

Mix half a tablespoon of veg-based oil and one tablespoon of dishwashing detergent in 16 ounces (500ml) of lukewarm water. Add to a spray bottle and focus on spraying both sides of the leaves. Spray this onto citrus trees once a week.

TIPS TO AVOID TRANSPLANT SHOCK

As I mentioned before, citrus trees can be pretty sensitive to a change in their conditions. You can expect to see *"some"* shock when transplanting your tree into the garden, but you can minimize the shock if you're careful. Some tips to follow are:

Be Gentle With the Roots

Avoid all contact with your citrus tree's roots unless they are root-bound. In fact, try to keep as much soil attached to the roots when transplanting as possible. Do not shake the earth free from the roots or bump the roots on anything.

Be Exceptionally Careful When Removing the Tree From the Pot

When easing the citrus tree out of the container, put a lot of time and effort into ensuring that the entire root system comes out with the tree. If the roots break off, you can expect the tree to have an adverse reaction to it.

Water the Tree Before Transplanting

Before you remove the citrus tree from its container, water it - this wets the roots and provides a good starting point. Ensure that the tree's roots remain moist for the entire process. If the tree's roots dry out (even a little), it will experience shock.

WARNING SIGNS OF POOR HEALTH OR TRANSPLANT SHOCK

A citrus tree will suffer transplant shock if it's unhappy with its relocation. In most instances, this is a temporary thing. The tree needs to re-establish its root system and have sufficient water and nutrition uptake to return it to a happy condition. Below are a few of the signs of transplant shock:

- Leaf scorch – this is the yellowing of the leaves between the veins and along the margins. The yellow section usually dries and turns crispy and brown
- Wilting leaves
- Leaf rolling/curling
- Sudden leaf loss

Tips to Overcome Transplant Shock

While you can't wholly avoid transplant shock, there are a few things you can do to create a pleasant experience for your citrus tree. Below are a few tips that I have found work quite well in helping a citrus tree settle into its new home.

Sweeten Things with a Bit of Sugar

A little bit of sugar can help to pep your tree up after a transplant. I like to apply a weak sugar water solution while transplanting as it can prevent transplant shock. This doesn't work every time, but it does most of the time, so it's worth trying.

Mix just one tablespoon of sugar in seven cups of lukewarm water and add this to the soil.

Trim the tree

Trimming back the tree by at least a third will be doing it a favor. When the tree has fewer leaves and branches to take care of, it can focus on growing and strengthening its root system. As a result, the tree gets stronger and recovers quicker.

Be patient

Many new citrus container gardeners panic when they transplant their citrus tree, and it doesn't respond well immediately. Avoid having a panic reaction. Don't add fertilizers or a multitude of soil enhancers. Provide basic care as you always do and wait it out. It can take a few days for the tree to recover. If you tamper with the tree too much, it could become even more shocked – and you don't want that.

SOIL REQUIREMENTS

While growing your citrus trees in pots, you have been in ultimate control over your tree's soil. When you transplant your trees into the garden, you can expect to lose some of that control. You can control it but to a lesser degree.

Citrus trees thrive in well-draining, sandy loam soils. If you find that you have heavy soil, you can improve it by adding compost and a few buckets of gypsum into your planting hole. It's imperative that the soil drains well, so ensure that you carry out the drainage test mentioned earlier.

SUN/SHADE PREFERENCES

Citrus trees love full-sun positions, but this poses a problem since you have protected your tree from the sun for some time. While a sunny spot is essential, think about transitioning your citrus tree before committing to the move. Move the tree in its container before transplant day. You can do this for several days before going ahead with the transplant.

Make a note of how the sun impacts the tree. You may need to provide a screen or some kind of temporary protection from the sun just until the tree gets used to the change in environment.

I've found that shade cloth provides the ideal amount of protection without completely shielding the tree from the sun. You will need to think of creating a frame for your shade cloth, though. Some people use a scaffold, but you can make a frame or use an old ladder opened over the tree – this depends on the size of your tree at the time.

You can also use a transparent spray on the tree. This should be available online or at your local garden center. This spray provides a thin protective film on the tree's leaves that deter water loss and protect the leaves while the tree gets used to full sun.

It's not a great idea to plant your citrus tree in shade or semi-shade. While the tree won't die, you will notice it producing more foliage and fewer flowers. In the end, you will have very few or no fruit.

PROTECTING A TRANSPLANTED CITRUS TREE IN WINTER

It's certainly not recommended to transplant a citrus tree into the garden in winter. It's safe to say that citrus trees don't enjoy the cold weather. If you have recently moved your citrus tree to the garden and it is just about to experience its first outdoor winter, there are a few things you can do to protect your tree from the elements.

Lemon and Orange trees are the most sensitive to the cold, while other citrus trees can be more cold-hardy. Still, the trees need protection. Here's what to do:

Boost the health of your tree

The healthier your tree is, the stronger it will be in the face of cold weather. Ensure that you fertilize your tree as required in the lead-up to winter and act promptly the moment you notice a tell-tale sign of disease or insect infestation.

Create a protective frame

You can make a frame that stands around your citrus tree and cover it in plastic. The frame should hold the plastic away from the tree's leaves and protect the tree from wind, rain, frost, and other changing weather conditions. If you can't make one, you should be able to buy one at your local garden center.

You have to keep an eye on the weather if you do this. If there's a sunny and warm day, you should remove the frame temporarily so that the heat and humidity within the plastic-covered structure don't build up. Here's how to make a protective frame:

1. Push four stakes into the ground around your citrus tree. Ensure that the stakes you use are tall, as they must be taller than your tree when pushed into the ground.
2. Connect the tops of each of the stakes with horizontal supports.
3. Place a layer of plastic over the top of the supports to create a canopy over the citrus tree. Use a big piece of plastic so that it drapes down over the sides of your tree.
4. Using staples or tacks, secure the plastic or material to the stakes. This will stop the plastic from falling down or blowing off in the wind.
5. Ensure that the plastic does not touch the citrus tree leaves as this can provide a freezing point.

Insulating the trunk and lower sections

If your citrus tree is already too big to cover with a frame and plastic, you can insulate the trunk and lower sections by wrapping the tree in foam rubber or fabric. Make an effort to get as much of the tree as possible covered.

Take the time to plan the transplanting of your citrus trees. The more prepared you are for the process, the more smoothly it will go.

Now that you're equipped to grow your citrus trees in containers and the garden, I'd like to spoil you with a bonus chapter on the gardening art (I like to call it that) of Espalier. Espalier is a type of gardening that has captured and attention and hearts of many creative gardeners across the globe. I strongly recommend trying it out for yourself. It's easy enough, and with your newfound citrus gardening knowledge, you should be able to nurture and care for a citrus Espalier just fine.

Turn to Chapter Eight for a bonus chapter dedicated to citrus Espalier gardening.

8

ESPALIER

M any people familiar with the appeal of Espalier want to know how to create their own. If you haven't heard about Espalier before, prepare to become obsessed. Creating an Espalier is not just gardening; it's art! Many people make the art of Espalier their hobby, and I understand why. For many years I would marvel over other people's Espaliers, and then finally, I decided to get stuck in and make my own. Creating an Espalier can teach you a lot about yourself because it demands time and attention, and nothing happens overnight – patience is key!

This chapter seeks to tell you everything I have learned about Espalier over the years, and as you might already have guessed, I include step-by-step instructions on how to get your own Espalier started. Starting with the basics of Espaliering will give you a good foundation to work from over the years.

First things first, what is Espalier? The image below depicts what Espalier typically looks like. This is one of many designs out there.

If you have ever seen what appears to be a wall of fruit trees growing vertically, then you've seen an Espalier. I find it interesting that Espalier is an ancient agricultural practice that's become popular for its aesthetic appeal.

In the Middle Ages, Europeans used Espalier to create dividing walls and separations in their communities. The structures were also grown inside castle grounds to produce fruit in a confined space without dealing with rambling fruit trees. The word "Espalier" is French and traditionally referred to the frame on which the fruit trees are grown/supported. Nowadays, the term only refers to the growing technique.

You may be wondering how it's possible to turn a woody citrus tree into Espalier, but it's a lot easier than you think. The trees are planted when they are very young saplings (usually before they are two years old). As the tree grows, the new branches are bent to shape and then secured to the frame, trellis, or wires positioned directly behind it.

By monitoring and bending branches to suit the design of the support behind it, the tree learns (and is aided) to grow in a particular configuration. Creating an Espalier isn't complicated, but it does take persistence, time, and patience. I poured a lot of myself into the creation of my own Espalier and in the end, I feel that makes all the difference. I think it's important to create an Espalier that portrays a little bit of your own personality – that's what I did with mine.

THE BENEFITS OF CITRUS ESPALIER

There are several benefits and reasons to love Espalier, some of which are as follows:

Espaliers are Aesthetically Appealing

The versatility of Espaliering is astounding – and what's even more astonishing is that *anyone* can do it. While Espaliers often appear in grand formal gardens, they can work in any space. Whether you're living in a city apartment with a balcony to use or a residential home with an average-sized garden space, Espalier can work!

Espaliers require a little more care and attention than regular trees, but once you have the knack for it, it becomes easy. I would go as far as to say that caring for your Espalier will become part of your routine. If you have a wall or trellised area, half the battle is already won as this is what your Espalier needs to survive and thrive!

And if you're wondering what patterns are possible for training your Espalier, you're in for a great surprise. You only need to pay a visit to Pinterest to find a wide variety of Espalier designs for you to consider. Many of these come with instructions, tips, and advice to help you along the way. Be warned; you may get lost in hours of scrolling if you start researching Espalier designs on Pinterest. Find a design you like (start with something simple to practice with) and get to work!

Espaliers are Practical and Space Saving

Many people give up on the idea of citrus gardening too soon because they don't have enough space for an orchard. At least that's what they think. It's good news that you don't need a lot of space to experience the joy of citrus tree gardening. With an Espalier, you can create a vertical orchard. You will save on space and have a practical area, making citrus tree care simpler and more manageable.

Espaliers Provide a Creative Focal Point/Feature

For me, the first draw to Espaliers was their aesthetic appeal. And I am aware that millions of other people across the globe appreciate the beauty of an Espalier too. That said, you can use an Espalier to create a focal point in your outside garden space. Another reason for growing an Espalier is that it can hide an unsightly wall. You can even create it to add value to your home – these are a sought-after feature!

Espaliering Increases Citrus Fruit Production

Of course, getting fresh fruit from the garden is a driving force behind so many people's interest in citrus gardening. Container gardening simplifies the citrus gardening process, but an Espalier takes it a step further. Such a feature creates a quick and convenient way to care for trees, and because they are set up and managed the way they are, they tend to provide increased fruit production. This is because Espaliers are set up against walls that reflect the sunlight a little more and retain heat at night, extending the season and allowing the fruit more time to mature.

Espalier Trees are Well Protected

As your citrus trees will be grown up against a wall, you can expect them to be safer from wind, rain, and other harsh elements. Your trees are also better protected from insect infestation (spraying them is a lot easier too).

Creating an Espalier

Before we jump into the steps of Espalier creating, let's look at a few things that need to be considered.

First and foremost, you need to be ready to support your Espaliered fruit trees throughout their lifespan. The central stem of your fruit tree needs to support several horizontal tiers with equal spacing. Most people aim for four or five tiers grown in a format that allows easy access to fruit. While Espalier is not complicated, it is high-maintenance, so you need time and patience. It can take up to five years to have a fully formed Espalier. To reduce the stress on you, limit how many citrus trees you choose to use.

You can encourage your citrus trees to grow into various patterns, from informal designs to more complex and trained designs. Some people make basketweaves, diamonds, or fanned patterns. For the sake of this instructional, we are focusing on creating a basic/simple tiered Espalier. It's better to get this right before you try something more complex.

Selecting Your Citrus Tree

Shop around for a citrus tree that would work in your Espalier – Limes and Lemons are especially rewarding in Espalier. Opt for a plant that has a small but strong, single stem. Alternatively, select a plant that has small side branches that you can prune off when planting.

Select Your Espalier Site & Plant Your Citrus Tree

Take the time to select the ideal site for your Espalier. A space with a simple background, an old wall, and even an old fencing frame is a good starting point. Remember that your citrus tree will enjoy full sun and well-draining soil. North and West facing walls generally provide the most amount of sunlight.

Ensure that you prepare the planting hole with compost and superphosphate to give your new tree a boost. You will have to plant the tree about 10in (around 25cm) away from the wall to ensure that the roots have enough space to grow and ensure that your tree has sufficient air circulation.

Getting the planting depth right is essential, so ensure that you settle your new citrus tree into the hole at the same depth that it was planted in its previous container. Once the tree is planted, water it well and add a layer of mulch around the tree, being careful not to let the mulch touch the actual stem of the tree.

Creating an Espalier Supporting Frame

Now that your citrus tree is settling into its new home, you need to focus on creating a supporting frame for it to grow on. For this, you will need heavy gauge (12 or 16) galvanized wire to create the frame. Keep the structure positioned around 6in (around 15cm) away from the wall.

Ensure that the first wire strand is approximately 15in (40cm) from the ground and then position each of the tiers at around the same distance apart. Drill holes into the wall with the measurements in mind, and use plastic plugs and eyebolts to attach your wire to the wall and secure it. If you prefer, you can build a wooden trellis that stands in front of the wall.

Pruning and Training

Now that your tree is planted and your frame is in place, it's time to focus on pruning and training your citrus tree to grow in the desired format.

Your first pruning is bound to be the most devastating for you – but don't worry; the pruning helps the tree grow stronger. The first pruning is done typically between late fall and late winter.

Below is an image showing how to begin training (and pruning your citrus tree).

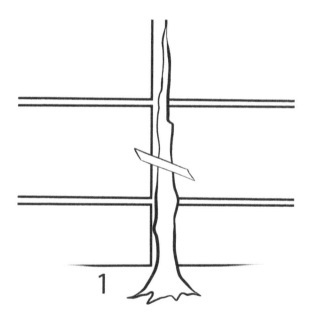

Prune the tree's main stem to 15in (40cm) in height. Try to cut the stem above three good buds (the central bud will extend the tree's size while the buds to the left and right will form the horizontal branches you will train).

When the summer comes around, you will need to focus on training the tree's central stem vertically. Keep manipulating the middle stem straight up. Train the right shoots and left shoots at 45-degree angles (as depicted in the image below) from the main stem.

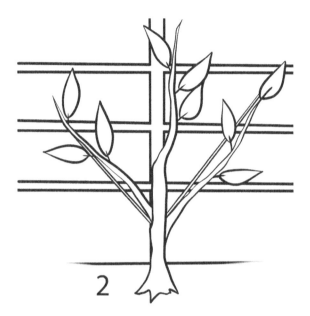

You can do a lot of your training using a soft string to tie branches onto wire strands gently. Ensure that you never tie the yarn onto the branches and shoots tightly as the tree grows at least double in diameter in a year.

When fall arrives again, it's time to start manipulating the lower shoots growing at a 45-degree angle. Gently lower the two lower branches and tie them to the first tier wire to branch them straight out from the main stem as shown in the image below.

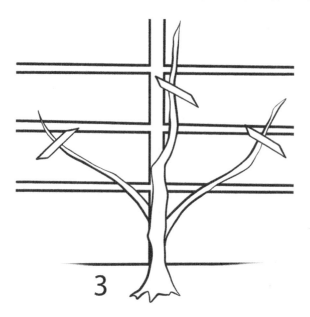

Cut the main stem down again to around 18in (46cm) from the lowest level, leaving three good buds as before. This is how the cycle starts again. Now only the lower two branches are extending directly outwards from the main stem.

When the tree's second summer arrives, it's time to focus on the horizontal branches one tier up from the lowest level. Select two branches (one left and one right) and secure them at 45-degree angles to the main stem, just as you initially did with the lowest tier when you started as shown in the image below.

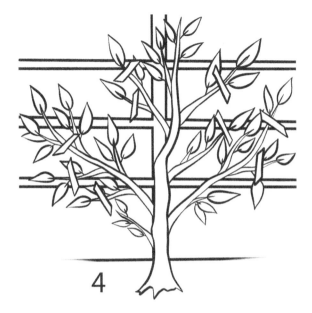

Prune all the branch shoots from the previous season down, leaving just three leaves per branch to the stem.

In the second fall, it's time to focus on the uppermost branches. Gently lower the uppermost branches and tie them to the second tier as shown in the image below.

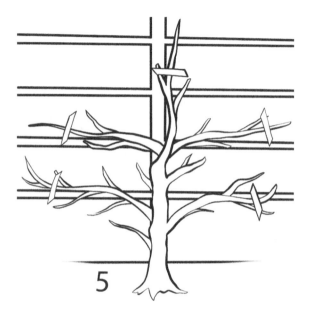

Prune at least one-third off the side branches and again cut back the central stem to 3 good buds, readying it for the next season.

Repeat this process each fall and each summer until the Espalier forms shape as depicted in the image below.

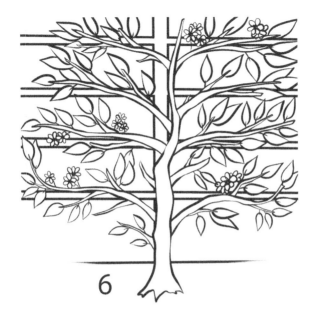

6

Then it's just a case of ongoing maintenance and pruning to remove undesirable growth and keep the Espalier's shape.

When your citrus tree reaches the top level of your desired design, wait until late spring and then cut back the new growths on the horizontal and vertical branches. This will stop the tree from growing any larger. In the summer, keep cutting back the shoots to three leaves to the main stem. This controls the overall size of the tree.

Tips for Espaliering Citrus Trees

When you first start Espaliering citrus trees, you are bound to have many questions. Below are a few tips aimed at newbies to this gardening artform. Select a sunny spot for your Espalier if you want thick green foliage and prolific fruit production. If you place your citrus Espalier in a shady spot, you can expect the vegetation to be dense, but the flowering and fruit production to be minimal.

- Fertilize your Espaliered citrus tree every second month during active growth, typically in spring and summer. During the winter and fall, fertilize the tree once every third month.
- Protecting your citrus Espalier in winter may be necessary. Creating your Espalier up against a sunny wall will help tremendously as the wall will trap heat from the sun and keep the tree relatively warm. You can also water the ground beneath the tree early morning so that the heat of the day can warm up the soil. Moist soil radiates more ground warmth than dry soil does.
- Use the right pair of pruning shears instead of a pair of scissors when working with your Espaliered citrus tree. Pruners can cut through thick branches without causing excess harm or damage to the stem. Do your tree a favor and use the right shears!

Now that you have a good basis for creating an Espalier, perhaps it's time to try making one of your own! Before you do, page onto our last section for a few last words from the author!

CONCLUSION

Having a passion for gardening is only part of what is required to be a successful citrus container gardener. Knowledge and know-how are just as important. I hope that this book has provided you with everything you need to pick up your gardening gloves and start citrus container gardening for yourself. It's a rewarding form of gardening that's close to my heart, and my dream is to inspire more people to give it a try.

I would strongly suggest gathering everything you need to get started before you attempt citrus container gardening. Gather the pots, compost, fertilizer, spray bottles, gardening gloves, containers, tables/shelves, trolley (for moving heavy pots around), and stones (to make a humidifier), pruners, watering cans, and of course, your trees or young saplings. By gathering all of this before you begin, you eliminate a considerable amount of potential frustration and hold-ups in the process.

Always remember that you can garden with this citrus container gardening handbook by your side. And if you have any indepth questions or need further guidance and advice, I am a mere email away.

To recap what we covered in the book, here are a few pointers to remember:

- Select your citrus tree type with care. Keep your climate, your space, and your own personality in mind when doing so. I recommend choosing one of the following: Kumquats, Lemons, Limes, Oranges, and Mandarins.
- Always use the correct type and size of pot. Plant your citrus tree, or sapling at the correct depth.
- When planting your citrus trees, ensure that you use the correct soil mix that's nutritional and well-draining.
- Familiarize yourself with general citrus tree care tips and techniques including watering, required temperatures, fertilizing, light requirements, pollination, and how to deal with common issues such as leaf drop.
- When moving your citrus tree inside/outside during the winter and summer months, do so in stages.
- Familiarize yourself with common citrus tree problems, and at the first sign of pests and disease, act swiftly and monitor progress after that.
- Take care when transplanting your citrus tree into the

garden – follow the instructions closely to protect the wellbeing of your tree.

- Pay attention to the weather conditions, and be prepared to provide your citrus trees with protection from the elements.
- If you choose to Espalier, be committed, patient and consistent.

You've made it – you're on the verge of becoming a successful citrus container gardener, and I am so pleased that I could help you along the way. Now you are ready to pick up your gardening spade, gloves, and pots and start creating your own citrus garden.

If you enjoyed reading this book, please leave a review on Amazon. It's through reviews and ongoing support that I can keep presenting content like this. Please scan one of the QR codes below, select your applicable country.

If you're based in USA:

If you're based in the UK:

Good luck!

REFERENCES

A. (2018, June 27). *How To Identify And Treat Citrus Tree Diseases And Insects*. Citrus.Com. https://www.citrus.com/blog/how-to-identify-and-treat-citrus-tree-diseases-and-insects/

Alternaria Leaf Spots - Google zoeken. (n.d.). Alternaria Leaf Spots. Retrieved 27 June 2021, from https://www.google.com/search?q=Alternaria+Leaf+Spots&client=safari&rls=en&sxsrf=ALeKk002WEtr01_FGWnaJPZrWXq7agjYuw:1624745071702&source=lnms&tbm=isch&sa=X&ved=2ahUKEwjIoeWGp7bxAhULgVwKHUFnA58Q_AUoAXoECAEQBA&biw=1395&bih=795

Anthracnose of Lime. (2021). Plantix. https://plantix.net/en/library/plant-diseases/100126/anthracnose-of-lime

Citrus canker - Google zoeken. (n.d.). Citrus Canker. Retrieved 26 June 2021, from https://www.google.com/search?q=citrus+canker&tbm=isch&ved=2ahUKEwio2_W1pLbxAhXTEWMBHfm1DUYQ2-cCegQIABAA&oq=citrus+canker&gs_lcp=CgNpbWcQARgAMgQIABBDMgIIADICCAyAggAMgIIADIC

CAAyAggAMgIIADICCAAyAggAOgQIIxAnOgcIABCxAxBDO gYIABAIEB46BggAEAoQGFDshQlY3aQJYKa0CWgDcAB4AIA BU4gByQWSAQIxMZgBAKABAaoBC2d3cy13aXotaW1nwAE B&sclient=img&ei=raHXYOjQDdOjjLsP-eu2sAQ&bih=795& biw=1395&client=safari

European brown rot citrus - Google zoeken. (n.d.). European Brown Rot. Retrieved 26 June 2021, from https://www.google.com/ search?q=european+brown+rot+citrus&tbm=isch&ved= 2ahUKEwikq9y7pbbxAhUu1-AKHXrSDtMQ2-cCegQIABAA& oq=european+brown+rot+citrus&gs_lcp= CgNpbWcQAzoGCAAQBxAeOggIABAIEAcQHjoGCAAQChA YUNueBlj9tAZgm7cGaABwAHgAgAFTiAHDCZIBAjE5mAEA oAEBqgELZ3dzLXdpei1pbWfAAQE&sclient=img&ei= xaLXYOS0Mq6ugwf6pLuYDQ&bih=795&biw=1395& client=safari

Fukushu. (2020). University of California Riverside College of Natural and Agricultural Sciences Citrus Variety Collection. https://citrusvariety.ucr.edu/citrus/fukushu.html

Fukushu or Changshou Kumquat. (2021). The Citrus Centre. https://citruscentre.co.uk/products/fukushu-or-changshou-kumquat?variant=19742354759

Freepik. (n.d.-a). *Caterpillar of a cutworm moth of the family noctuidae on a sweet basil plant of the species ocimum basilicum 11873182.* Retrieved 26 June 2021, from https://www.freepik.com/ premium-photo/caterpillar-cutworm-moth-family-noctuidae-sweet-basil-plant-species-ocimum-basilicum_11873182.htm

Freepik. (n.d.-b). *Freepik | Discover the best free graphic resources about citrus tree in garden, 1,435 results.* Retrieved 26 June 2021, from https://www.freepik.com/search?dates=any&format= search&page=4&query=citrus+tree+in+garden&sort=popular& type=photo

Freepik. (n.d.-c). *Freepik | Discover the best free graphic resources about mealybug, 10 results*. Retrieved 26 June 2021, from https://www.freepik.com/search?dates=any&format=search&from_query=mealybug&page=1&query=mealybug&sort=popular

Freepik. (n.d.-d). *Snail on a green leaf 13659437*. Retrieved 26 June 2021, from https://www.freepik.com/premium-photo/snail-green-leaf_13659437.htm#page=2&query=snail%20on%20leaf&position=37

Freepik. (2019, November 11). *Fungus rust of lime. 6011264*. https://www.freepik.com/premium-photo/fungus-rust-lime_6011264.htm#page=1&query=citrus%20mite&position=0

Freepik. (2020, September 14). *Detail of an aphid infestation, aphididae, feeding on the sap of a plant. 10078581*. https://www.freepik.com/premium-photo/detail-aphid-infestation-aphididae-feeding-sap-plant_10078581.htm

Grant, A. (2020a, February 20). *Lemon Tree Problems: Treating Common Lemon Tree Diseases*. Gardening Know How. https://www.gardeningknowhow.com/edible/fruits/lemons/common-lemon-tree-diseases.htm

Grant, A. (2020b, April 11). *Controlling Citrus Scale – How To Treat Types Of Scale On Citrus Plants*. Gardening Know How. https://www.gardeningknowhow.com/edible/fruits/citrus/controlling-citrus-scale.htm

Grant, A. (2020c, November 4). *Controlling Citrus Scale – How To Treat Types Of Scale On Citrus Plants*. Gardening Know How. https://www.gardeningknowhow.com/edible/fruits/citrus/controlling-citrus-scale.htm

Grant, A. (2021, February 14). *Sweet Lime Varieties – Sweet Lime Tree Growing And Care*. Gardening Know How. https://www.

gardeningknowhow.com/edible/fruits/lime/sweet-lime-tree-growing.htm

Alternaria Leaf Spots - Google zoeken. (n.d.). Alternaria Leaf Spots. Retrieved 27 June 2021, from https://www.google.com/search?q=Alternaria+Leaf+Spots&client=safari&rls=en&sxsrf=ALeKk002WEtr01_FGWnaJPZrWXq7agjYuw:1624745071702&source=lnms&tbm=isch&sa=X&ved=2ahUKEwjloeWGp7bxAhULgVwKHUFnA58Q_AUoAXoECAEQBA&biw=1395&bih=795

Greasy spot citrus - Google zoeken. (n.d.). Greasy Spot Citrus. Retrieved 26 June 2021, from https://www.google.com/search?q=greasy+spot+citrus&tbm=isch&ved=2ahUKEwj31Y-ApbbxAhVs0uAKHQq6AXAQ2-cCegQIABAA&oq=greasy+spot+citrus&gs_lcp=CgNpbWcQAzICCAAyBggAEAgQHjIGCAAQCBAeOgQIIxAnOgQIABBDOggIABCxAxCDAToFCAAQsQM6BggAEAUQHjoECAAQGDoECAAQHlDPrwdYjMgHYMPJB2gBcAB4AIABV4gBxgqSAQIxOZgBAKABAaoBC2d3cy13aXotaW1nwAEB&sclient=img&ei=SKLXYPeRM-ykgweK9IaABw&bih=795&biw=1395&client=safari

Alternaria Leaf Spots - Google zoeken. (n.d.). Alternaria Leaf Spots. Retrieved 27 June 2021, from https://www.google.com/search?q=Alternaria+Leaf+Spots&client=safari&rls=en&sxsrf=ALeKk002WEtr01_FGWnaJPZrWXq7agjYuw:1624745071702&source=lnms&tbm=isch&sa=X&ved=2ahUKEwjloeWGp7bxAhULgVwKHUFnA58Q_AUoAXoECAEQBA&biw=1395&bih=795

J. (n.d.-a). *Espalier Tree On Old Wall Stock Photo (Edit Now) 143213965.* Shutterstock.Com. Retrieved 27 June 2021, from https://www.shutterstock.com/image-photo/espalier-tree-on-old-wall-143213965

Alternaria Leaf Spots - Google zoeken. (n.d.). Alternaria Leaf Spots. Retrieved 27 June 2021, from https://www.google.com/search? q=Alternaria+Leaf+Spots&client=safari&rls=en&sxsrf= ALeKk002WEtr01_FGWnaJPZrWXq7agjYuw: 1624745071702&source=lnms&tbm=isch&sa=X&ved= 2ahUKEwjIoeWGp7bxAhULgVwKHUFnA58Q_AUoAXoECAE QBA&biw=1395&bih=795

K. (n.d.-b). *Citrus Leaf Miner Damage On Lime Stock Photo (Edit Now) 1091450861.* Shutterstock.Com. Retrieved 27 June 2021, from https://www.shutterstock.com/image-photo/citrus-leaf-miner-damage-on-lime-1091450861

Kumquat Tree Care: How to Grow Kumquats. (2020, June 17). Epic Gardening. https://www.epicgardening.com/kumquat-tree/

Leigh, E. (2018, November 28). *How Long Does it Take for Oranges to Grow on a Fully Developed Tree?* Homeguides SFGate. https://homeguides.sfgate.com/long-oranges-grow-fully-developed-tree-59477.html

Limequat. (2021, March 17). Wikipedia. https://en.wikipedia. org/wiki/Limequat

Limequat "Tavares." (2016). Lubera Fruitful Gardening. http:// www.lubera.co.uk/plants/mediterranean-plants/citrus-plants/ limes/limequat-tavares

Mandarin oranges. (2021). Plant Village. https://plantvillage.psu. edu/topics/mandarin-oranges/infos

Phytophthora Gummosis citrus - Google zoeken. (n.d.). Phytophthora Gummosis citrus. Retrieved 26 June 2021, from https:// www.google.com/search?q=Phytophthora+Gummosis+citrus& tbm=isch&ved=2ahUKEwj2qLD1orbxAhVF0RoKHZIuClsQ2- cCegQIABAA&oq=Phytophthora+Gummosis+citrus&gs_lcp= CgNpbWcQAzICCAAyBggAEAgQHjoECAAQHjoECAAQGFD

QVljZX2DMYWgAcAB4AIABTIgB2gOSAQE3mAEAoAEBqg
ELZ3dzLXdpei1pbWfAAQE&sclient=img&ei=
GaDXYLa4GsWia5ndqdgF&bih=795&biw=1395&
client=safari

QR Code Generator – create QR codes for free (Logo, T-Shirt, vCard, EPS). (n.d.). QR Code Generator. Retrieved 26 June 2021, from https://goqr.me

Sooty mold fungus citrus - Google zoeken. (n.d.). Sooty Mold Fungus. Retrieved 26 June 2021, from https://www.google. com/search?q=sooty+mold+fungus+citrus&tbm=isch&ved= 2ahUKEwihy9P7orbxAhUH-BoKHYO4C1sQ2-cCegQIABAA& oq=sooty+mold+fungus+citrus&gs_lcp= CgNpbWcQAzoECCMQJzoICAAQsQMQgwE6BQgAELEDOg IIADoECAAQQzoGCAAQBRAeOgQIABAYOgQIABAeUOyqF 1iX4hdgs- QXaABwAHgAgAFXiAHLC5IBAjI0mAEAoAEBqgELZ3dzLXd pei1pbWfAAQE&sclient=img&ei=JqDXYKGgJIfwa4PxrtgF& bih=795&biw=1395&client=safari

T. (n.d.-c). *Common Brown Scales Colony Sucking Citrus Stock Photo (Edit Now) 511478410*. Shutterstock.Com. Retrieved 27 June 2021, from https://www.shutterstock.com/image-photo/ common-brown-scales-colony-sucking-citrus-511478410

Tolliver, K. D. (2020). *How to Germinate Sweet Lime Seed*. Home- guides SFGate. https://homeguides.sfgate.com/germinate- sweet-lime-seed-43162.html

Skaria, R. (2018, April 29). *Citrus Container Takeaways:* Us Citrus. https://uscitrus.com/blogs/citrus-simplified/the- container-choice

A. (2021). *Oranges and Lemons*. The Gardener. https://www. thegardener.co.za/grow-to-eat/diy-food/oranges-lemons/#:~: text=BEST%20CONDITIONS%20FOR%20CITRUS%

20TREES&text=The%20soil%20should%20be%20well,(brack)%20are%20not%20recommended

Boeckmann, C. (2021). *GROWING LEMONS & ORANGES PLANTING, GROWING, AND HARVESTING CITRUS FRUITS.* The Farmers Almanac. https://www.almanac.com/plant/lemons-oranges

How To Grow Citrus Trees. (2021). Stodels. https://www.stodels.com/how-to-grow-citrus-trees/

HOW TO GROW CITRUS TREES IN CONTAINERS. (2019). Pennington. https://www.pennington.com/all-products/fertilizer/resources/growing-container-citrus-fragrance-fruit-and-fun

IONESCU, F. L. O. R. I. N. A. (2021). *How to Grow a Lemon Tree from Seed | Step-by-Step Guide.* You Had Me At Gardening. https://youhadmeatgardening.com/lemon-tree-from-seed/#:~:text=Wrap%20the%20seeds%20in%20a,current%20date%20on%20the%20bag

Ellis, M. E. (2019, August 26). *What Is A Pebble Tray – Keep Plants Humid With A Pebble Saucer.* Gardening Know How. https://www.gardeningknowhow.com/houseplants/hpgen/what-is-a-pebble-tray.htm

Skaria, A. (2020, October 13). *GROW LIGHT FOR CITRUS TREE: 3 KEY FEATURES TO LOOK FOR.* Us Citrus. https://uscitrus.com/blogs/citrus-simplified/grow-light-for-citrus-tree-3-key-features-to-look-for#:~:text=Full%2Dspectrum%20lighting%20is%20going,stage%20of%20the%20plants%20growth

Viljoen, M. (2019, March 18). *14 Things Nobody Tells You About Indoor Citrus Trees.* Gardenista. https://www.gardenista.com/

posts/13-things-nobody-tells-you-grow-indoor-citrus-trees-lemon-lime/

A. (2017, August). *Growing Citrus Indoors*. Plantscapers. https://plantscapers.com/growing-citrus-indoors/#:~:text=If%20indoors%20where%20an%20air,it%20the%20humidity%20it%20loves

A. (2020). *How To Care For An Indoor Orange Tree*. Smart Garden Guide. https://smartgardenguide.com/indoor-orange-tree-care/

Buckner, H. (2019, December 23). *GROWING CITRUS INDOORS: CREATE A LITTLE SLICE OF PARADISE*. Gardeners Path. https://gardenerspath.com/plants/fruit-trees/grow-citrus-indoors/#:~:text=Growing%20Tips,-Provide%20at%20least&text=Keep%20indoor%20temperatures%20between%2055,in%20light%20exposure%20or%20temperature

Carroll, J. (2021). *Kumquat Tree Care: Tips For Growing Kumquat Trees*. Gardening Know How. https://www.gardeningknowhow.com/edible/fruits/kumquat/growing-kumquat-trees.htm#:~:text=As%20part%20of%20your%20kumquat,thereafter%2C%20following%20the%20label%20instructions

Crane, J. H. (2019). *HOW TO GROW AND CARE FOR AN INDOOR LEMON TREE*. Pennington. https://www.pennington.com/all-products/fertilizer/resources/how-to-grow-and-care-for-an-indoor-lemon-tree#:~:text=Always%20leave%20a%20few%20inches,too%20wet%20or%20too%20dry

de Jauregui, R. (2019, November 4). *How to Fertilize Citrus Container Plants Home Guides | Garden | Soil Care*. Home Guides.SFgate. https://homeguides.sfgate.com/fertilize-citrus-container-plants-57703.html

M. (2021). *Lemon (Container Grown) Growing Guide*. Grow Veg. https://www.growveg.co.za/plants/south-africa/how-to-grow-container-grown-lemons/

Slatalla, M. (2019, December 6). *Winter Is Coming: How to Keep an Indoor Citrus Tree Happy*. Gardenista. https://www.gardenista.com/posts/winter-is-coming-how-to-keep-an-indoor-citrus-tree-happy/

A. (2021). *Greasy Spot*. Plantix. https://plantix.net/en/library/plant-diseases/100125/greasy-spot

Caring for Citrus in Fall. (2017, October 16). UCANR. https://ucanr.edu/blogs/blogcore/postdetail.cfm?postnum=25440

Citrus Diseases and Disorders of Leaves and Twigs. (2016). UC IMP. http://ipm.ucanr.edu/PMG/C107/m107bpleaftwigdis.html

European brown rot, rotting fruit, techniques and treatments to avoid and cure the disease. (2021). Nurture & Garden. https://www.nature-and-garden.com/gardening/european-brown-rot.html

Grant, A. (2019, August 26). *What Is Citrus Canker – How To Treat Citrus Canker Symptoms*. Gardening Know How. https://www.gardeningknowhow.com/edible/fruits/citrus/what-is-citrus-canker.htm

Lynn, A. (2020). *Mealy Bugs On Citrus*. Home Guides SF Gate. https://homeguides.sfgate.com/mealy-bugs-citrus-26552.html

Ritcher, R. (2015, July 6). *Citrus Leaf Miner*. Texus A&M Agrilife Extension. https://agrilife.org/harrishort/2015/07/06/citrus-leaf-miner/#:~:text=Citrus%20leaf%20miner%20damage%20to%20leaf.&text=This%20insect%20is%20a%20tiny,winding%20pathway%20through%20the%20leaf

Scale Insect. (2021). Planet Natural Research Centre. https://www.planetnatural.com/pest-problem-solver/houseplant-pests/scale-control/

Stillman, J. (2011). *HOW TO IDENTIFY AND CONTROL ANTHRACNOSE.* The Old Farmers Almanac. https://www.almanac.com/pest/anthracnose

Waterworth, K. (2021, April 1). *Citrus Fruit Brown Rot: Tips For Brown Rot Control On Citrus.* Gardening Know How. https://www.gardeningknowhow.com/edible/fruits/citrus/citrus-fruit-brown-rot.htm#:~:text=article%20should%20help.-,Citrus%20Fruit%20Brown%20Rot,garden%20fungal%20pest%2C%20Phytophthora%20spp.&text=Brown%20Rot%20of%20citrus%20fruit,that%20have%20a%20potent%20smell

A. (2020, August 26). *Protecting Citrus Trees from Cold.* Sunday Gardener. https://www.sundaygardener.net/protecting-citrus-trees-from-cold/

Rhoades, H. (2020, September 9). *Learn How To Avoid And Repair Transplant Shock In Plants.* Gardening Know How. https://www.gardeningknowhow.com/plant-problems/environmental/learn-how-to-avoid-and-repair-transplant-shock-in-plants.htm

Signs of transplant shock and what to do. (2021). Blerick Tree Farm. http://www.blericktreefarm.com.au/wp-content/uploads/2017/08/Signs-of-Transplant-shock-and-what-to-do-to-avoid-it.pdf

Skaria, A. (2020, April 30). *4 EFFECTIVE HOMEMADE ORGANIC PESTICIDES FOR CITRUS FRUIT TREES.* Citrus Us. https://uscitrus.com/blogs/citrus-simplified/4-effective-homemade-organic-pesticides-for-citrus-fruit-trees

Transplanting Citrus Trees Takes Care and Effort but Can be done. (2017, July 3). Daily News. https://www.dailynews.com/2017/

07/03/gardening-transplanting-citrus-trees-takes-care-and-effort-but-it-can-be-done/

A. (2021a). *Fruit Tree Espalier.* The Gardener. https://www.thegardener.co.za/grow-to-eat/fruit/fruit-treeespalier/#:~:text=Training%20fruit%20trees%20into%20an,value%20and%20increased%20fruit%20production.&text=A%20wall%20reflects%20more%20sunlightmature%20and%20extending%20the%20season

Akimkina, I. (2021, May 3). Espalier [Illustration]. In *Espalier.*

How to espalier like a pro. (2021, March 11). Better Homes and Gardens. https://www.bhg.com.au/how-to-espalier

McCullough, N. (2021). *USING ESPALIERS IN THE GARDEN.* Garden Design. https://www.gardendesign.com/trees/espaliers.html

T.E.E.B. (2021b). *Espalier.* Britannica. https://www.britannica.com/topic/espalier

Green, J. (2021, May 10). *Potting Soil* [Growing Citrus in Containers]. Facebook. https://www.facebook.com/groups/1682879975276072

McGhee, M. (2021, May 10). *Potting Soil* [Growing Citrus in Containers]. Facebook. https://www.facebook.com/groups/1115584552172929

Made in the USA
Las Vegas, NV
27 August 2023

76705571R00095